A Different Calling

A Manual For Lay Ministers

Kenneth P. Langer

Brass Bell Books

BRASS BELL
BOOKS & GAMES

Published by Brass Bell Books and Games
www.brassbellbooks.com

Printed in the United States of America

Love never ends or fails. Love never ends. Everything must be based on love–the relation between two friends, my ministry, my service; the church services in every field must be based on love. Why? Because God is love.
POPE THEODOROS II

Contents

Introduction

What Does It Mean to be a Lay Minister?

T he word minister has a Latin root that means to be a servant. A servant of what? The answer to that comes from looking at the word minister not as a noun but as a verb. To minister means to attend to someone's needs or to provide something necessary or helpful. A minister works to help others who are in need of spiritual, physical, mental, or emotional assistance in their lives. There are many specific ways in which a minister can provide this kind of help. He or she can be a counselor; a listener; an advisor; a spiritual guide; a leader of ceremonies, services, and rituals; someone who offers blessings and consolations; a teacher, mentor, retreat leader, or a role model, just to name a few. Traditionally, a minister is a person who has undergone special education and training in a specific spiritual tradition and who has been ordained or specially recognized through that tradition.

A lay minister is someone who feels a calling or a need to help others but, for whatever reason, does not or cannot undergo the intense training needed to become an ordained minister. Lay ministers occasionally perform some very similar functions to a minister but are not usually paid. Often they are members of a volunteer helping organization or are members of a religious practice led by a minister or professional leader. Lay ministers often provide support to the work of a minister or to the mission of a charitable organization.

Both ministers and lay ministers do many different things but the central idea is to help other people through care and compassion. The purpose of this book is to divide those and other functions into four main roles: Spiritual Advising, Spiritual Direction, Sacred Circles (gatherings), and Sacred Retreats and to provide tips and lessons for doing each of these functions without a great deal of prior training. Each section will include helpful information and both solo and group exercises. At the end of the book is a complete outline of all the chapters for study. All of these concepts are presented so that they can be practiced by people of any religious or spiritual tradition which can serve as a foundation of care and fellowship.

Chapter One: Spiritual Advising

Introduction

S piritual Advising is the ability of a lay minister to offer advice and non-professional counseling to others in a spiritual context. While some traditions call this ability pastoral counseling, the term that will be used here is Spiritual Advising.

A counselor is defined in dictionaries as one who counsels or gives advice but the word counselor has come to connote in our society one who is a specially trained and licensed therapist. The type of counseling discussed here is not professional therapy nor is it meant to replace any form of professional therapy. If a person is in need of professional help then he or she should get that help. Spiritual Advising is about how to offer spiritual advice to people who want someone who can use spiritual ideals to help him or her solve problems or overcome immediate life challenges.

Spiritual Advising is a short-term interaction between a lay minister and a person who seeks advice. (I will call this person a Seeker throughout the book rather than a client or advisee.) The Seeker often is in need of advice in order to overcome a particular challenge in life or wants to find help in solving a question or dilemma. The emphasis of the help session led by a Spiritual Advisor is on the Seeker's need to resolve a spiritual or life issue. The Spiritual Advisor does not teach, coach or lead the Seeker in any way. Instead, he or she will help the Seeker be heard or find a path to follow and will do so primarily by encouraging the Seeker to help herself.

Main Reasons People Seek a Spiritual Advisor

- *Facing a difficult change*
- *Facing a life transition*

There are many reasons why people seek advice from friends, spiritual leaders, or professional counselors. Many of these reasons revolve around the fact that life is filled with changes and these changes can result in difficult challenges. As creatures of nature who seek safety in known environments and habitual patterns, change can be met with a wide range of resistance. Some can adapt to change when necessary but, at some point, all of us will encounter resistance to difficult changes in life.

It can be very helpful to have someone aid us through such times. People in such situations will often turn to a friend or loved one for guidance and those relationships can be very valuable and helpful but there are other times when a person who is more skilled at leading someone through a difficult challenge is needed. It is at these times that people often seek out help from a Spiritual Advisor because dealing with many of these changes requires one to weigh spiritual considerations. It is through our spirituality that we derive our view of the cosmos and our place within the universe and it is this view that can help us find our way through difficult times.

Many of the changes we encounter in life have to do with the transitions that are a part of the cycle of living and dying. All humans experience the natural stages of youth, adolescence, adulthood, and old age. Each of these stages involve a fundamental change to one's view and place in the society and the world. Other changes are voluntary but equally challenging. Marriage, children, and finding a career are just some of the many difficult choices that are encountered in life. Still, other things can happen to force change upon our lives such as natural disasters, accidents, loss of a job, abuse or violence, a change in viewpoint or personality, or any number of other unforeseen events.

Not being able to make adjustments due to these changes can lead to further problems such as anxiety, depression, guilt, or grief which can further challenge our ability to deal with a new reality. All religious traditions offer ways in which people can deal with these changes. In a free society, each person is free to choose his or her own theological viewpoint and can use that spirituality to help find ways to deal with life's troubles. Lay ministers can act as guides through the thickets of those challenges.

The purpose of this section is to provide guidance for training in providing Spiritual Advising for people of all spiritual traditions and practices.

Notes on This Chapter

This chapter of the book will be focused on one-on-one advising between a single advisor (the Spiritual Advisor) and an advisee (the Seeker). In order to have a balance of gender pronouns, I will refer to the Advisor in the feminine and to the Seeker in the masculine and will continue that practice throughout most of the book.

There are several exercises in the book to help people practice their skills as a Spiritual Advisor. Some can be done individually but many require having at least one partner with whom you can practice. These exercises could be done in a class setting where members of the class take turns practicing with different partners. Some exercises will require discussing real or imagined advising scenarios. A class or team should prepare some likely situations before doing the exercises.

The Relationship

Introduction

Spiritual Advising is usually done between two people: one who seeks advice in dealing with a difficult change or challenge and believes that the solution to that problem is spiritual, and another person who is skilled both as a spiritual mentor and a guide. The two will form a unique relationship that is different from the ones with parents, friends, or other social bonds.

Imagine this: You just moved into a new house or apartment. You've settled in and are ready to begin a new phase in your life. One night, though, you hear strange sounds in your basement. You have not been in the basement very much because it's a dark and creepy place–even in the daytime. You decide to ignore the sounds but they come back. In fact, they keep returning night after night and each time they get a little bit louder and more disturbing. You know you cannot afford to move out or go somewhere else and you cannot go on living with this frightening anomaly in your house so you decide that you have to do something about this problem. Going into the basement seems too scary and dangerous so you make a decision to open the door to the basement just a little and wait to see what might come out from down below.

Evening comes and the sounds begin. You walk to the basement door and open it then you sit back from the door and wait. Sound scary? Now, what if you had someone there who once had similar problems in her basement and had come over to your house to sit with you? She could calm you down and help you through that difficult time. The two of you might develop a supportive relationship. You know you could come to depend on her to help you defeat the demons that may rise up from the dark stairway.

It takes a certain kind of person to be willing to seek help from another and it takes a certain kind of person to be willing to offer that help. The type of relationship that those two develop will be different from other relationships. The experience of being in an advising relationship is similar to what someone might experience with a friend sitting by the open door to that dark basement.

The Spiritual Advisor

The Spiritual Advisor is a unique person. She wants to help others without an expectation of payment or thanks. She gives of herself freely and is willing to enter into uncomfortable situations. A person like that must have patience, compassion, and a basic understanding of the complexities of being human in a challenging world.

Qualities of a Spiritual Advisor

- *Compassion*
- *Inner strength*
- *Confidence*
- *Acceptance*
- *Empathy*
- *Patience*
- *Trustworthiness*

Spiritual Advisors also need a certain amount of inner strength. They need to have delved deeply into their own personal issues and come to terms with their own inner demons so that when someone comes to her with a challenge, the process of overcoming that challenge will not be unfamiliar to the Advisor. The Spiritual Advisor need not have experienced every ill in the world in order to know how to overcome them but the experience of facing and surmounting a personal challenge will prove invaluable to her when asked to help another.

An important factor of inner strength is personal confidence. Confidence has a "Catch-22" quality to it. You need to have confidence in order to act with conviction but confidence is only built from having a history of success. The way to develop confidence and to assure future success in your advising practice is to always be honest with yourself and others about your ability, to practice your skills slowly–with guidance–and to develop an attitude that allows you to make and build upon your mistakes.

Spiritual Advisors must also possess a particular attitude toward others. A socially phobic curmudgeon would find spiritual advising to be particularly challenging. Advisors need to be open and warm toward others so that an atmosphere of acceptance and security is created during the advising session. Spiritual Advisors need to accept the individual value and worth of every person. Seekers can have a low opinion of themselves and of their own ability to heal. Spiritual Advisors help those seekers find that inner worth and show them how to use it as a tool to overcome problems. Advisors are successful at this only if they deeply believe that all people possess an innate ability to succeed.

Spiritual Advisors also need to be empathetic. Empathy is often confused with sympathy but they are really two different things. Sympathy means to be in tune with the feelings of another because one has experienced those same feelings. Some string instruments have sympathetic strings or strings that vibrate when other strings are plucked. The sympathetic string vibrates because it shares qualities possessed by the plucked string. Similarly, a sympathetic person can understand the feelings of another because he or she has experienced similar feelings. The ability of an advisor to be sympathetic allows her to relate to personal experience in order to help another.

Sympathy can have a negative connotation, however. Though one person may have experienced the same pains as another, the fact that she has already defeated that demon can instill in her a sense of false superiority. In this way, sympathy can turn into pity and become detrimental to the healing process.

Empathy is different from sympathy because it requires one to be in tune with the pain of another even though that pain has never been personally experienced. This is a much more challenging and different personal quality to develop and nurture. It requires one to expand the personal experience of pain to a greater level. Through developing empathy, all suffering becomes universal. The empathetic person can relate to all inner turmoil without regard to the individual circumstances that cause the suffering. Such a person does not shy away from pain but seizes the opportunity for growth that suffering often contains. The empathetic Spiritual Advisor knows that there is no growth without adjustment and that growing can sometimes be painful.

Patience is yet another important quality needed for a Spiritual Advisor. Growth happens in its own time and this is even more true for the growth of others. Advisors must give seekers the room to grow and explore. Even though the solution to a problem may be painfully obvious to an advisor it will be meaningless to the Seeker until it is personally discovered (albeit through the guidance of the Advisor). The patient person is tolerant and is willing to take on some short-term discomfort or frustration in order to wait for a desired long-term result.

The patient person has enough inner strength to withstand the negativity of others and is able to see through that negativity into the suffering that often manifests it.

Along with patience, the Spiritual Advisor must also be trustworthy. The Seeker must feel safe enough to be willing to share inner personal feelings and know that those feelings will be respected and not shared with others. In order to overcome pain, difficult feelings and emotions must be allowed to be exposed and explored. This requires that the Seeker be open and vulnerable. Without trust and confidentiality, the space needed to allow these things to rise up from the inner depths will not exist and growth will be impossible.

Sacred Listening

Introduction

The most important skill for any Spiritual Advisor to learn is the skill of Sacred Listening. Sacred Listening is different from just hearing and ordinary listening. Hearing (for those who are able to hear) is an ability. We hear all the time (even when we are asleep) but we do not always listen. Listening happens when we pay attention to what we are hearing.

Sacred Listening is a special kind of listening. Not only does the Sacred Listener pay attention to what she is hearing, she gives full and complete attention to the person speaking. Furthermore, she does not listen as an individual waiting for her time to speak. She listens as an ear to the condition of the world around her. The life story of the Sacred Listener is not important. It is the story of the Seeker and his search for healing that is all important.

The Sacred Listener also has an ability to hear beyond the words. She waits patiently for clues to the problem and possible avenues of exploration to reveal themselves in either clear or veiled ways. In the very act of Sacred Listening, the listener exudes a sense of caring and calm and lets the Seeker know that what he says is worthy of being heard. The Spiritual Advisor knows that the Seeker is a sacred being who is trying hard to reach that sacredness and become whole. Through all the pain, frustration, and anger there is a connection to life that is trying to break through and that will need to be reflected in the words of the Seeker as he speaks.

In the true sense of the word, Sacred Listening is just that: listening–and little more. In the act of Sacred Listening there is very little conversation. The listener does not offer solutions, make helpful comments, or offer many insights. She just listens and makes the Seeker feel accepted and heard. There is great healing power in just listening. For some people who feel they have never really been heard, a Sacred Listener is a blessing. Some people have been talked to all of their lives with little chance given to be heard themselves. There is always someone with an opinion out there of what we should do. By just listening, we empower someone and let them know that they are valued.

Listening tells someone that their words and ideas are important and may even encourage them to begin their own search for balance. To just listen, to really just listen, can be very challenging, though. It demands of the listener that she get past her own ego and offer the Seeker the gift of pure attention. It is natural for a caring person to want to help by trying to offer solutions or to offer what may seem like the best answer to a problem but the truly needed answer may not be the one that we offer. The right solution, more often than not, is the one that the Seeker finds in the process of putting words to his thoughts.

Talking makes us verbalize our thoughts, feelings, and emotions. Sometimes the very process of being given the space to organize and talk through a tangle of confused feelings helps one to better understand those feelings and, in the process, begin to see a way clear through them. Sacred Listening encourages people to explore and gives them the space to begin a search for answers.

Sacred Listening does sometimes involve asking questions but those questions are designed only to help the Seeker find ways to explore and express his thoughts more fully. Questions are asked only when the Advisor feels that the oration of the Seeker has come to the point at which the Seeker needs some encouragement or direction to continue. The questions are short and open-ended and call upon the Seeker to think and reflect on the answers. In responding to those questions, the Seeker is encouraged to think out loud and express any feelings that may be uncovered in the process. The true art of a good Spiritual Listener is to know when to listen, when to ask questions, and when to be silent. The focus of Sacred Listening must be first and foremost on listening even if that means listening to silence and to ask questions only when absolutely needed.

The Process

The Sacred Listening Process
• *Preparation* • *Preview* • *Listening* • *Review*

If possible, the Sacred Listening session should begin with a bit of preparation. Careful preparation of a session might not always be possible, however, since Sacred Listening can take place anywhere and at anytime. You might come across someone at the store or coffee shop and a serious conversation could begin. A Spiritual Advisor will recognize cues in the conversation that the person talking is really seeking help and a Sacred Listening session may ensue. However, many times a session will be planned in advance and the Advisor can make some preparations.

The Preparation

Foremost in importance, the session needs to be in a private, safe, and comfortable environment and the Seeker needs to feel secure within that environment. The room should be small and have comfortable chairs in which to sit. It should be closed off so that others will not be able to hear. All possible distractions such as phones and televisions should be shut off. Any other possible nuisance should be removed, if possible. The decor of the room should give off a sense of warmth and relaxation. Depending on your spiritual tradition, you can begin the session with a brief ritual or prayer or the lighting of a candle. Allow the space used for the session to become a sacred space for you will both be doing spiritual work.

Before beginning any session, it is important to discuss some limitations with the Seeker. This is often a difficult part of the process for some Spiritual Advisors but it is very important and can save you from mistakes and difficulties in the future. Sometimes, as advisors, we want to appear as if we are capable of helping anyone and that all our sessions will be wonderful moments of healing and joy but this is just not always the case.

As an Advisor, you are responsible for protecting both yourself and the Seeker and clearly outlining limits at the beginning of a session is a way to do that. One such limit for consideration is time. The Advisor needs to tell the Seeker how much time she is willing to devote to listening. More than an hour is often too much. Secondly, if it is apparent that more than one listening session is needed, the advisor should determine how many times they will meet in total. Spiritual advising is a short term limited activity unlike other activities such as professional psychotherapy, life coaching, or spiritual direction. Anyone needing more than a few sessions of Sacred Listening may need to seek help from or be referred to a professional counselor.

The Advisor should also discuss her own limitations. If you have little experience doing this work than that fact should be stated. Most people are very understanding about this. Even if you have lots of experience in Sacred Listening, it is important to let the Seeker know that you are not a professional counselor and that you have not had that kind of training (unless, of course, you do have that kind of training).

Part of creating an atmosphere of safety and comfort comes by assuring the Seeker that everything discussed will be kept confidential. A Seeker must feel free to reveal very personal and private feelings and thoughts. He will not be able to do that if he thinks that what he says may become tomorrow's gossip. The relationship between an Advisor and Seeker is a sacred one and it is made sacred through trust. There are, however, necessary limits to confidentiality and these, too, must be discussed early on in the session.

Several court cases have proven that the confidential nature of a therapeutic relationship has legal limits and counselors have been sued when those limits were crossed. Instances when the Seeker has raised the possibility of danger to himself or to others or where situations of abuse, illegal activity, or other types of harm are discussed, the advisor is under a moral and legal obligation to report the information to proper authorities. The best way to avoid any of these difficult situations is to be very clear at the onset of a session that confidentiality will be maintained as long as there is no legal or moral conflict. Failing to do this, the Advisor should clearly warn any Seeker that may begin to have such a discussion that she, the Advisor, is obligated to report any such conversation to the appropriate authorities. The Seeker is then given the chance to continue or end the conversation with full knowledge of the possible consequences of continuing.

The Preview

The next step is to do a very brief preview of the situation before engaging in a complete discussion. Ask for a brief general explanation of the situation. From this general description you should be able to do a quick assessment of whether or not there may be a problem with the limits to confidentiality mentioned above. Also, you can make an assessment as to whether or not you are truly capable of helping. This will be a personal judgement based on experience, on an honest evaluation of your personal abilities, and on an ability to be open about your own limitations to others. There will be some challenges where you may be helpful and there will be others where you might not be so helpful. The Spiritual Advisor will most likely be helpful with situations that involve spiritual questions or that deal with mild emotions, life transitions, or basic life challenges but will likely be less successful with problems that may be deeply rooted and require years of professional help. The Advisor should encourage the Seeker to find help from other professionals that involve financial matters; legal matters; issues of mental, physical, or emotional illness; or (as mentioned earlier) any situation which may involve a danger to the advisor, the Seeker, or anyone else.

In many other therapeutic relationships, a client goes to a counselor's office in some other location away from home. The counselor is often a stranger to the client and the relationship is purely professional. The separation between counselor and client is clear and distinct. Relationships with Spiritual Advisors are often not as clear. Advisors tend to members of some spiritual community and may be friends with the Seeker before they enter into an advising session. The advantage to this reality is that the Seeker will know the Advisor and may already feel confident and secure in meeting with her and the Advisor may already have some understanding of the Seeker's situation. The disadvantage is that entering into a confidential advising relationship may change or even put a severe strain on any preexisting friendship. There is some amount of distance that needs to be established in advising and that distance may feel awkward in an already close relationship. In doing the initial assessment, the Advisor should consider what effect this conversation may have on the relationship of the person who has now become a Seeker.

Active Listening

After the preview, it is time to begin the actual listening. When I speak of listening I am talking about the art of Active Listening. You may be familiar with the comedic image of the husband who sits at the breakfast table, reads his paper, and mumbles "yes, dear" as she incessantly talks away. The husband may hear the wife in this fictionalized situation but he is surely not listening. In a typical conversation between friends, two people may be listening but they are often also thinking about what they will next say to each other. Active Listening is being fully engaged in the act of listening. Active Listening involves three components: listening, confirming, and encouraging.

Active listening is the ability to be open to the person to whom you are listening through your mind, heart, and body. Active

Listening is similar to being in meditation in that it is necessary for you to clear your mind of all distracting thoughts so that you may focus solely upon your goal. Try not to judge, analyze, or categorize what you hear. The heart, too, must be open and free to experience and feel. This can be done by avoiding the natural tendency to compare others by your own standards. As long as no harm or threats are intended in their words, be accepting of what you may hear. Develop an empathetic heart that can understand the feelings of others. Accept that the feelings the Seeker is speaking about are real and genuine to him.

Be open with your body by adopting a listening position that signals to the Seeker that you are truly interested in what he is saying. Try not to cross your arms or legs. Instead, engage the Seeker in a relaxed position. Face the Seeker directly and look at him; make eye contact often. It can also help to adopt a particular hand position while engaged in sacred listening. Buddhists call a special hand position used during meditation a mudra. It can be something very simple like touching your index finger to your thumb. I often use a position in which I put my hands together with my fingers interlaced except for my index fingers which are raised slightly and pointed forward. This mudra serves to remind me where my focus of attention should be placed as I listen.

Let your soul also be open to the Seeker and allow the listening to become a truly sacred act. In the preparation phase, you may have either overtly or discreetly created a sacred space. Within that space, open your soul so that you feel a deep connection to your own conception of divinity. Allow yourself to become a conduit of care that fills that sacred space. Once again, it is not your job to fix every problem that the Seeker may reveal to you but you can allow yourself and your caring to be available to your Seeker. That energy comes first from your own heart as you accept and care for the Seeker but it is fed from the source of all love, healing, and care. Before considering doing any kind of healing work such as Sacred Listening, it is important that you have your own personal understanding of that mysterious source and that you find ways to draw upon it. If the energies of love and healing are available to the Seeker and, together, you both find ways to open up his channels of love and healing, he will be able to use those as he needs. Listen to your feelings and intuition as the Seeker speaks.

A large part of doing Sacred Listening is in learning to be silent. The natural urge of any caring person is to try and fix the problem for someone else. Seemingly, this would end the problem and make the caring person look like a hero but the quick fix is often not the best solution. True change can never come from the outside. The motivation for change and the strength and drive needed to make a change must come from within. A person needs to "own" their realization so that the drive to succeed is genuine. As an Advisor, resist the urge to speak except when words are really needed to encourage the Seeker to continue their journey. Try not to "fix" the problem even if you think the solution is simple and obvious. Be unafraid of moments of silence. In everyday conversation, silence is avoided and people can feel uncomfortable in that silence but a hushed moment can be just what is needed in a Sacred Listening situation. Silence gives room for someone to consider their thoughts and feelings. Silence can urge people to elaborate and talk through their feelings without any need for encouragement.

Non-Verbal Messages
• *Tone of voice*   • *The face*   • *Body position*   • *Bodily movements*

- _Unusual changes in standard patterns_

The Sacred Listener also needs to develop the skill of non-verbal listening–understanding the messages sent by the Seeker without any words. Non-verbal listening is an important part of Sacred Listening and is the reason that advising is difficult to do when not in the presence of the Seeker. We communicate a lot of information through our voices and bodies and all of that information is part of what needs to be heard by the Spiritual Advisor.

Non-verbal information is read by carefully observing the actions, sounds, and movements of the Seeker and can often confirm what is felt intuitively. Through our bodies we constantly send information about our feelings and attitudes. The true meaning and intent of our words is often revealed more through our actions than our words. People can say one thing but their bodies often know the real truth even if the mind has been fooled to believe something else. Part of the job of the Sacred Listener is to observe the body of the speaker and hear its messages as well. A Seeker's words may directly conflict with his body language.

When a Seeker speaks, he not only elicits words but the way in which those words are delivered can say a great deal. The Advisor should listen for specific word choices and how they are delivered. The tone of voice will reveal additional information. Listen to the range of the voice and how high or low the words sound in comparison to his normal voice range. Listen for shakiness in the voice, words that break up or crack, or words that are heard to hear. Listen for the speed of the delivery. All of these factors and more can indicate tension and anxiety. People who are relaxed and at ease with themselves will usually speak at a fair pace with an even quality to their voice. All speech contains natural inflection which is a rising and falling of tone and pitch but an excited person speaks with a greater range of pitch and tones. Listen to hear what the normal speech patterns of the Seeker sound like, especially in the early assessment phase, and then listen for variations in that pattern later in the session. Changes in regular patterns can help the body to illustrate a particular emotion or can indicate that the words being spoken are not in line with what the body is feeling. In the act of Sacred Listening the advisor does not share this information with the Seeker. Instead, she attempts to get the Seeker to explore those feelings with just a few short questions so that she can continue the process of listening.

Similarly, information can be gained by carefully observing the face of the speaker. Look for changes of color in the cheeks, forehead, ears, and neck; lines and veins that may appear; and flaring of the nostrils. The mouth can also express a lot of information through a smile, frown, or grimace; by changes in the corners of the mouth; or by a pinching or rolling of the lips. When the body knows that the words being revealed do not express true feelings, the speaker often tries to hide that in the face which can cause tension and slight nervous motions. Degrees of anger, fear, frustration, and other emotions can leak their way out in the many small muscles of the face. The eyes, too, can reveal a lot of information. Crying and sobbing are obvious signs of distress and hurt but smaller signs are also possible. There may be redness in the eyes, the size of the pupils may change, or there may be excessive blinking.

Sometimes the Seeker has fooled himself to the point that his face may be still but the tension caused by strong emotions often come out in some other part of the body. Learn to observe the whole body and all its positions and movements. Check to see if the person is slouching or sitting straight. Look to see the direction to which his body and head are facing. We often look unconsciously toward what we seek. Check to see if the arms are open or closed defensively. Also observe the legs for the same amount of openness. Are they crossed or resting comfortably?

Take note of the position and direction of the head. Look for rhythms in the body such as twitching or tapping fingers, moving hands, swinging or jiggling feet or legs, and movements of the upper body caused by strong or shallow breathing.

The most important clues, however, are not specific positions or motions but changes in those actions. Part of the purpose of the preparation before a serious discussion begins is to get the Seeker to relax and feel comfortable which allows the Advisor to observe how the Seeker sits and moves when relaxed. Variations in those things help give the Advisor information on how the Seeker actually feels about the words being spoken.

Another important part of Active Listening is to confirm to the Seeker that you are actually listening and that you are interested in what he is saying. This can be done with short verbal confirmations such as an occasional "uh-huh" or "I see." Again, Sacred Listening must focus upon listening and calls upon the listener not to ask a lot of questions or engage in a great deal of discussion. A few simple words that let the Seeker know you have been listening carefully and with full attention are all that is often needed. Confirmation can also be done with physical actions such as leaning forward toward the Seeker, smiling, or nodding as the Seeker speaks. Other body motions or positions should be kept to a minimum so as not to distract the Seeker.

Confirmation
• _Verbal_ • _Physical_ • _Attitude_

Though these are obvious ways of letting the Seeker know you are interested in what he is saying, the most important part of confirmation, however, is less obvious–at least to the naked eye. A necessary part of confirmation is the attitude of the person doing the listening. If you are not listening to the Seeker or are not truly interested in what is being said then that will eventually be detected. Just like the Seeker's body may tell a story, so will the listener's body. People can tell when someone is not focused upon their words. More than that, though, we are all capable of detecting the level of attention directed toward us. Your attitude and degree of caring will be reflected in the amount of attention that you direct towards the Seeker. You have to truly be interested in what the Seeker is saying and care about his desire for wholeness.

Encouragement

- *Silence*
- *Brief questions*

The act of Sacred Listening includes the ability to encourage the Seeker to further the conversation when it seems that it has hit a proverbial roadblock. The focus of Sacred Listening is listening, of course, but sometimes the Seeker may get "stuck" and have nothing to say. Encouragement should only be done when the advisor is certain that the Seeker needs some help in furthering his dialogue. Often, the inexperienced Advisor will jump in too early to fill awkward moments of silence. It is useful to try and resist the urge to instantly rescue the Seeker from discomfort. Sometimes just being silent is encouragement enough. Silence allows people to collect their thoughts and to have some room to explore inner feelings. A calm hushed moment can make people naturally want to elaborate on what has just been said. There is a certain call to truth in the quiet that can be more powerful than any spoken words. The Seeker can use silence as a powerful tool but doing so requires a certain strength and patience that comes with self-control, experience, and self assurance.

Types of Questions

- *Encourage continued exploration*
- *Check on feelings*
- *Check on thoughts*
- *Spiritual connection*

If a Seeker seems truly stuck and several moments of silence are ineffective then it may be time to try a short word of encouragement or to ask a brief exploratory question which will help the Seeker find a way to continue. Short phrases like "go on," "continue," or even "I'm listening" may be enough to help the Seeker break through the invisible barrier he has encountered. At other times a short question is needed to focus the Seeker's mind. Since Sacred Listening is centered mainly on listening, any questions asked should be sparse and rare. Questions that should be used will focus only on encouraging the Seeker to continue talking about the situation. Those kinds of questions fall into four categories for an Advisor: those that help to move the story along, those that help the Seeker check in on feelings, those that help the Seeker check in on his thoughts, and those that help the Seeker explore a spiritual connection to his situation.

Questions like "What happened next?" "Can you tell me more about..." or "What did you mean when you said...." can help the Seeker focus on in on a particular part of his story in order to encourage him to keep him talking and exploring. They can also serve to redirect a Seeker back to the main issue if he tends to drift off into other non-related subjects. Some Seekers may seem more cerebral or more emotional than others. It helps to have them find a careful balance between thoughts and feelings.

For those that need more exploration of feelings, questions like "How did you feel about..." or "How did that make you feel when..." help the Seeker focus on his feelings and emotions in relation to his story while questions like "What did you think about...." or "What went through your mind when..." can put the emphasis of the discussion on thoughts. In order to keep the listening sacred, it is helpful to occasionally ask questions that reminds the Seeker of his spiritual connection. Questions like "how do you see this situation in light of your spiritual tradition?" or "how does this affect your spiritual life?" help center the conversation on the role of the Seeker's spiritual connection to the universe and to others and helps the Seeker view the situation in a wider context.

Review

- *Summarize*
- *Close*

The final part of Sacred Listening is called the review. In this stage, the Seeker's oration is still the focus of the session but instead of being allowed to continue he is asked to begin to bring the session to a close by reviewing what has been said and discovered. In essence, the Advisor asks the Seeker to think back on the entire conversation and briefly summarize what has been said–distilling what may have been an hour of talk into a few minutes of review. The Seeker should focus on the healing and growing aspects of what was learned and revealed as much as possible and the Advisor should encourage him to do that with brief reminders or questions.

As much as is possible, the session should end on a positive note so that the Seeker feels that he has accomplished some small amount of movement toward wholeness even if that movement was made possible by just being heard. The Advisor may close the session by thanking the Seeker for sharing his story and by affirming that she believes in his ability to work through his situation. A person may feel very vulnerable and exposed after having revealed such personal feelings and may need to be reassured and comforted. Finally, the ending discussion may revolve briefly on what the next step should be, if any.

Listening To Yourself

So far, we have focused on developing the ability in Sacred Listening to listen to another person. Equally important is to develop the ability to listen to yourself as part of the process.

<u>Self Listening</u>

Self listening occurs during the Sacred Listening with the Seeker. It makes the process of listening more challenging because you have to listen to more than two people: the Seeker as well as yourself. As a Sacred Listener you need to be empathetic with the Seeker but you also need to check in with your own feelings and reactions to what is being said. The Sacred Listener does this for some of the same reasons that she listens and watches for actions and reactions of the Seeker. The body of the listener can also reveal information about what is being said.

The listener must first make sure that she is remaining relaxed and focused while listening. If tension arises in the body of the listener it is important to try and discover the reason for that surge of energy. What is the Seeker saying that causes you to react? Is there something he said that relates to you and your life situation? If so, you may need to call upon your own memories and feelings to see what is going on. You may be able to relate to the same problem from experience or you may be discovering something within yourself that may need attention later. The

Seeker is not the only one who may experience growth within a Sacred Listening session.

The Sacred Listener needs to occasionally check in with her own body throughout the session. Begin with checking the breath. Breathing should be slow and relaxed as you listen. If the breathing becomes fast or shallow, then something emotional has been activated and the listener needs to pay attention to feelings or thoughts that may arise. Just as you observed the words, vocal tone, and face and body movements of the seeker, so should you monitor your own words and actions as you listen and interact with him. Your powers of awareness and intuition may be detected best from within your own body and its motions and reactions. Pay attention to any and all the feelings that arise within you. It is important to recognize whether or not the feelings come from within the self or are prompted by the Seeker.

Checking in with your own feelings and with your intuitions and abilities means also maintaining an open mind throughout the session. What you may be hearing may not be exactly the real situation. Most of the time that may be because the Seeker is not trying to intentionally mislead you as much as he may be trying to mislead himself. If he is comfortable in the session and feels that he can trust you not to be judgmental then he will have no reason to try and appear to be different from what he is. Years of being shaped to conform by society or parents and friends, however, may lead him to try and keep the truth of his inner reality from himself. We all try to live up to certain social expectations and cultural assumptions and may try to convince ourselves of a false reality concerning them. Listen carefully to what the Seeker says but also be willing to adjust what you hear with the reality being defined by his reactions and by your own reactions. With time and patience and a belief in the worth and strength of each person, the path to wholeness will eventually be revealed.

Exercises

The following are several exercises designed to help you increase your skills as a Sacred Listener. The first set of exercises are meant to be done alone and the second set of exercises should be done with a partner. The partners should take turns being both Listener and Seeker. After completing the partner exercises, the two participants should take some time to talk about what each person did well and what could be done to make the session more helpful and effective.

Solo Exercises

Solo Exercise no. 1 - Listening To Yourself

The goal of this exercise is to get you to feel comfortable in just listening. If you can begin to listen carefully to yourself then you will be able to listen to others.

- Sit comfortably in a quiet spot where you will not be disturbed.
- Set a timer for one minute.
- Close your eyes.
- Quiet your thoughts.
- Listen to the sounds within your body:
  1. your breath
  1. your heart
  1. the blood in your veins
  1. the high pitch sound of your nerves

Repeat the exercise several times increasing the time limit. Try to get to five minutes.

❋

Solo Exercise no. 2 - Listening To Your Surroundings

This exercise is designed to get you to listen to everything beyond yourself.

- Sit comfortably in a place that has some existing noises.
- Set a timer for one minute.
- Close your eyes.
- Quiet your thoughts.
- Listen to all the sounds of the environment around you. Try to identify each of the separate sounds and then hear everything together as one cacophonous sound.

Repeat the exercise several times increasing the time limit. Try to get to five minutes.

❋

Solo Exercise no. 3 - Observing Body Movements

Body movements can often suggest additional information to the words being spoken by a Seeker. In order to practice watching the body movements of a speaker it is important that the speaker does not know that he is being observed for this purpose.

- Watch several videos about body language.
- Watch a video of someone speaking or attend a live lecture. Listen less to the words and more to how the words are being delivered and spoken. Take notes on what you see and hear.
- Observe the facial expressions of the speaker. Pay attention to the eyes and lips as well as to other parts of

the face.

- Observe the position and movements of the body. Pay attention to the hands and feet and other motions in the body.

Partner Exercises

Partner Exercise no. 1 - Being Comfortable With Silence

After becoming comfortable with silence by yourself it will be time to find that same comfort level in the presence of another person. Our society teaches us not to be at ease when we find ourselves with others in moments of silence. We instinctively try to find something to say to fill the void. This exercise is meant to help you break that instinct and to be calm and relaxed while silent with another person. Both people should sit comfortably fully facing each other with hands resting comfortably in their laps.

Begin by looking at each other's hands. As you look, concentrate on relaxing your body and opening your mind. After at least one minute, both of you should look at each other's throats and neck area. Again, concentrate on relaxing and remaining open. After another minute, look into each other's eyes. Remain open and relaxed. Resist the temptation to look away and be protective. See the person both as a struggling individual and as a sacred being.

�֍

Partner Exercise no. 2 - Sending Comfort To Another

Part of the role of the Sacred Listener is to help the Seeker feel at ease while moving toward wholeness. With this exercise you will practice sending that comforting energy to your partner. Face each other and sit comfortably. Begin by having both people close their eyes with hands folded gently in their lap. Each person should concentrate on their breathing. As you breathe in, draw in calming breaths. As you exhale, experience a feeling of calm. Both should now open their eyes and continue to focus on the breath. Allow the hands to open with the palms facing toward your partner. As you breathe, allow your feeling of calm to expand until it includes your partner. Look into your partner's eyes and remain calm and relaxed for several minutes.

✳

Partner Exercise no. 3 - Confirming

In this exercise, one person should speak about a real or imagined situation. The other person should practice listening carefully without interjecting. As the speaker talks, the listener should practice using confirming sounds and gestures. Have one person (the speaker) begin talking. As the speaker talks the listener should listen quietly while paying complete attention to what is being said. The listener should occasionally use confirming sounds and motions as described earlier in this chapter such as "uh-huh," or "I see." Be careful to use these judiciously so that they remain genuine and affirming and not distracting. When done, discuss the exercise and then switch roles.

✳

Partner Exercise no. 4 - Short Questions

The emphasis on this exercise is to practice using short questions that encourage the listener to keep the story moving while still focusing primarily on listening. Have one person begin talking about a real or imagined situation. The listener should listen carefully to what is being said. At various times, the speaker should introduce pauses into the conversation at which time the listener should decide whether or not to maintain the silence (an encouragement in itself) or ask one of the following short questions:

1   What happened next?

1   Can you tell me more?

1   How did that make you feel?

1   What did you think about that?

1   How does that relate to your spirituality?

When done, discuss the exercise and then switch roles.

�֍

Partner Exercise no. 5 - Sacred Listening

In this final exercise of this section the pair can practice putting all of the previously learned skills together. Have one person talk about a real or imagined situation. The listener should make sure that she has an open and caring listening posture. A listening mudra can also be used by the listener. During the conversation the listener should concentrate on listening fully and carefully to the speaker. While listening, the listener should also be aware of and comfortable with moments of silence and send comforting energy toward the listener. Pay careful attention to the tone, choice of words, and quality of sound made by the speaker. Observe movements of the body and face. Use confirming sounds and gestures. Use silence or ask short questions to keep the conversation moving. When done, discuss the exercise and then switch roles.

Spiritual Advising

Introduction

Spiritual Advising and Sacred Listening are similar ways to offer help to someone experiencing a challenge in life. They are both short term treatments and are focused on temporary difficulties encountered in life. They both seek to intervene in order to offer the Seeker a way to find changes and solutions in his life and they both focus primarily on the needs and motivations of the Seeker. The difference between Sacred Listening and Spiritual Advising is that Spiritual Advising is more proactive. The Advisor is more involved in helping the Seeker search for a solution.

All advising sessions should begin with Sacred Listening and move into Spiritual Advising only when the Seeker indicates the need for additional intervention. In all cases, it must be the Seeker who signals the shift from one method to the other. In many cases, listening is all that the Seeker needs and desires and the Spiritual Advisor must resist the natural caring urge to do more. Seekers who engage a listener will often begin a process of helping themselves release inner feelings and discover their own solutions. They simply need validation and encouragement. Patience on the part of the listener is often the most valuable advising tool she can have.

Cues to the Need for Spiritual Advising

- *Asking for help*
- *Sacred Listening has not helped*
- *Emotional upheaval*
- *Falsity*

There are at least four major cues that indicate that the Spiritual Advisor should move from the mode of Sacred Listening to the mode of Spiritual Advising. The appearance of any one of these cues by itself should not immediately signal the Advisor to move into an advising stance. Sacred Listening should be encouraged for as long as is possible and patience will be required of the Advisor to allow things to unfold naturally. If, however, any of these cues begin to occur repeatedly or there is a combination of cues, then it may be time to move on to more intervention in the session.

The first cue that may signal a need for change in approach is that the Seeker asks for help. Of course, the fact that the Seeker has come to you for advising in the first place is a call for help but the process of Sacred Listening is focused on the idea of allowing the Seeker to help himself by working through the challenge aloud. If the Seeker does not eventually come to feel some progress, however, he may become frustrated and ask for more help. The call for help may be verbal or it may be a complete change in body posture and attitude.

A second cue occurs when the Sacred Listening session comes to a complete halt. The Seeker becomes stuck and cannot go on regardless of how many confirming signals and how much verbal encouragement you offer. The Seeker may hit the proverbial brick wall and be unable to move forward in any way.

A third cue is if the Seeker becomes too involved with his emotions as he speaks which causes an emotional upheaval. In this case, the emotions take over and the ability to think clearly and speak effectively is hampered. If this happens, the Seeker must first be given the chance to calm down and begin again but it may be impossible for him to do so.

The final cue is more subtle and requires careful vigilance by the Advisor. If the words of the Seeker clearly do not match the non-verbal signals being sent, then there may be falsity. In other words, the Seeker is not being true to himself. If such a condition goes on for a long period of time, the Advisor may need to intervene and carefully point out the inconsistency. The level of intervention will be based on the level of falsity and may require a switch to the Spiritual Advising mode.

The process of moving someone toward a different view is similar to the process of climbing a steep mountain or exploring a mysterious land. Someone who wishes to do such exploring will often seek out a guide–a person who knows the territory and can lead him. In Spiritual Advising, the Seeker is the explorer and the Advisor is the guide. The Advisor does not take the journey for the Seeker. Instead, she simply points the Seeker in the right direction and follows along in case more help is needed. The Seeker is the one who leads the adventure.

Techniques

- *Define the problem*
- *Explore feelings*
- *Relate to a spiritual connection*
- *Define concrete actions*

The first part of the session will be focused on defining the problem in clear and concrete terms. Many times the Seeker will seem to be faced with a multitude of problems each of which is wrapped up in deep and confusing emotions. Often, however, what appears to be a myriad of challenges can be pared down to a few primary concerns. One of the goals of the session will be to help the Seeker find these fundamental causes to his difficulties.

The next part of the session will be used to help the Seeker root out and explore his feelings related to this core situation. The Advisor should encourage the Seeker to discuss, examine, and live out these emotions. People often bury emotional feelings deep inside themselves in order to appear "normal" and strong when, in reality, inner strength can only be gained by bringing emotions to the surface. Emotions exist for a reason and are not simply annoyances in a perfectly controlled life. They exist to help us protect ourselves from dangers and to aid us in working through difficult changes.

The third phase of a session will focus on defining and using the Seeker's spiritual connection to gain strength in working toward a solution. It has been said that most problems are spiritual problems. Spirituality is about finding and enriching your connection to things beyond yourself and it is those things that we need to depend on to be strong and whole. The Spiritual Advisor is unique among helpers because she is allowed and expected to talk about spiritual matters.

The final part of the session is in defining and enacting concrete actions that can be done to help the Seeker make changes for the better. Recurring problems in a person's life can be brought upon by many things including, but not limited to, certain triggering events, habitual actions, or destructive attitudes. Part of a good plan for overcoming challenges will include steps that can be taken to avoid those triggers and to change those habits and attitudes. A concrete plan will also include goals for the Seeker to accomplish and a method for evaluating the effectiveness of the plan, which may include additional sessions with the Advisor.

Note that this is all a very logical progression of steps. Rarely, however, does a session actually unfold in such an orderly fashion. You may find that the session moves toward different aspects of these four areas and in different degrees though having these four areas in mind does help to keep the session on track. If the session does get off track, the Advisor may need to redirect the conversation back toward one of these areas.

The way to get a Seeker to reveal information about these four areas is to encourage him to have a full and frank discussion with you. There are four techniques that can help an Advisor lead a Seeker through a worthwhile and helpful advising session.

Guiding a Session

- _Listen_
- _Observe_
- _Take notes_
- _Try to clearly define the problem_

One way the Advisor can help the conversation stay on track is to take notes during the session. Notes about problems, feelings, and spiritual connections can be jotted down so that if the Seeker begins to move away from these areas of discussion the Advisor can remind herself of the issue at hand. Cues given in words or body movements can also be noted so that the Advisor can ask questions about them when there is a chance to do so. Notes can also help you review the session and serve as a reminder for any future sessions with that person. Reviewing past notes can also help you learn how to do future sessions better.

If you decide to take notes be sure to ask the Seeker first for permission. Remember that anything you write down can be taken as evidence in any future legal proceedings. I suggest that you not write the Seeker's name anywhere in the notes but find another way to refer to the session. Even writing the time and date could lead back to the Seeker. When taking notes, it may be helpful to actually mark four large spaces with one of the four areas listed at the top giving you room to put in notes about problems, feelings, spiritual relationships and possible solutions.

Clearly Defining The Problem

One of the most difficult tasks in a spiritual advising session is to help the Seeker define the actual problem. Often the Seeker will come to you with a long list of challenges each of which is connected to one or more deep feelings. Since Spiritual Advising is meant to be a short term solution, it is important to try and pare away the list of difficulties.

Searching For the Problem

- *Listen*
- *Paraphrase*
- *Ask meaningful questions*
- *Share stories and information*
- *Offer advice*

The goal is to try and find one or two core issues that can help resolve most, if not all, of the other problems. These core challenges must be defined in very concrete terms so that they can be faced fully and openly. The way to find these core challenges is to encourage the Seeker to discuss his situation and, through that conversation, guide him toward finding the central issues.

We have already seen how Sacred Listening is fundamental to all advising sessions. The process of Spiritual Advising begins with Sacred Listening as well in the hopes that the Seeker will guide himself to a solution. When it becomes clear that this is not going to happen then it is time to move on to other techniques. One such technique is paraphrasing, which is when the Advisor condenses and repeats back to the Seeker what he has just said. Paraphrasing has two purposes. One, the Advisor can be sure that she has heard the Seeker correctly and lets the Seeker know that she has heard him. Two, it lets the Seeker hear his thoughts and ideas in a new way. Sometimes we are not aware of what we are really saying until we hear our own words come back to us. With paraphrasing, long thoughts and sentences are reduced down to a short idea that is shared with the Seeker. The Seeker is then able to clarify as to whether or not the paraphrasing accurately describes his situation. Paraphrasing helps to narrow down a discussion until key elements can be identified.

To learn how to paraphrase, you need to practice listening to people talk and pay attention to the people, events, and emotions mentioned in their words. When these things have been identified then repeat back what you heard in a condensed form while you emphasize the people, events, and emotions that were mentioned. Begin the paraphrase with an opening statement such as: "Let me see if I understand this, you said....." or "What I hear you saying is...." or "It sounds to me as if...." After the paraphrase is complete, the Advisor then asks to see if her interpretation is correct–allowing the Seeker to make any corrections. It is important to remember that paraphrasing is reducing and reiterating what the Seeker has said and nothing more. The Advisor must resist the urge to pontificate, make speeches, pass judgment, or do anything else that would change the nature of the paraphrase.

Questioning Techniques
<ul><li>*Make them infrequent*</li><li>*Make them open-ended*</li><li>*Make them short and simple*</li><li>*Start with who, what, when, where, and why*</li><li>*Focus on the most significant details*</li><li>*Do not demand an answer*</li></ul>

Another technique that can be used is to ask questions. Questions should be asked infrequently and only when they are needed to clarify or gain additional information. Questions need to be open-ended, not yes or no questions, which encourage the Seeker to think and reveal more about his situation or talk more about his feelings. Sometimes people use questions to actually manipulate others into coming around to their way of thinking or to control a conversation. These kinds of misleading efforts can be avoided if questions are kept short and simple and are focused on information and exploration only. Such questions can start with simple phrases such as: "Can you tell me more about...." or "What did you think about....." or "How did it make you feel when..." These kinds of questions begin with the five questioning words: who, what, when, where, and why and are always set in the positive such as in: Why did you feel the need to...." instead of "Why didn't you..." or "What did you think about..." instead of "What didn't you understand about...."

Questions should help the conversation move from the general to the specific which can be done by focusing on the most significant factors and details identified by the words of the Seeker. The Advisor must be careful to listen to these specific words and be ready to ask for more information about them. In this way, the Advisor is not leading the conversation through questions but is allowing the Seeker to always lead the discussion. The Advisor simply fleshes out additional thoughts and feelings which gives the Seeker even more material to explore. Sometimes Seekers will not have an answer to a question or are not ready to face an answer. In such cases, the Advisor should not insist on an answer. A forced answer will simply cause the Seeker to withdraw or may even cause him to feel uncomfortable with the whole session.

Another technique that can be used to further a conversation is to share information or stories with the Seeker. As with questioning, this technique should be used sparingly and only when needed to keep the Seeker moving forward in his personal exploration. Information should be shared only when the Seeker either implicitly or directly asks for it and only basic information should be given. This should not be a time for the Advisor to demonstrate her immense knowledge on a particular subject of interest. The Spiritual Advising session is for the benefit of the Seeker and not the Advisor. Information is given because the Seeker has asked for it and so he can use that knowledge to continue his journey. Information should be given in that light only. Sharing stories about yourself is a way of transmitting information and sharing experiences. Seekers can sometimes take comfort in knowing that the Advisor has had similar difficulties or challenges but, again, stories should only be shared if they benefit the present conversation. Stories and information shared should be free of conflicts and should always be positive.

Even though I have chosen the term Spiritual Advisor, actual advice should very rarely, if ever, be given out. Giving advice assumes that you have the one and correct answer to a situation. Even if the proper solution seems to you to be obviously clear it is unwise and, possibly, detrimental to offer that solution to the Seeker as outright advice. One's answer may turn out to be another's dilemma. The true answer for the Seeker will be the one that he eventually discovers with your help. It may be the very same answer you envisioned during the conversation but it will be his answer then and not yours. He will be able to embrace it as his own and be ready to move forward to make positive changes. Advice should be given only when it is absolutely needed as an intervention to prevent further unavoidable difficulties.

The techniques of listening, paraphrasing, questioning, sharing, and advising all help the Seeker to flesh out more information and discover greater depth to the situation he is describing. The objective of getting this information is to try and determine what central issue or issues are at the core of the situation. Since Spiritual Advising is a temporary short term activity, it is crucial to focus on one or two particular problems so that a solution can be sought. There are some additional techniques that can be used to help someone do just that.

Additional Advising Techniques
• *Identify areas of control* • *Look for causes*
Triggers *Environments*
• *Explore feelings*

First of all, the Seeker needs to learn to separate the things that are under his control from those that are not. There are things we can change in the world but there are many more that we cannot. Most of the things that we can have influence over involve our own selves. If we can identify a need for change within ourselves we can then focus on how to make that change. We cannot change things beyond our own control and trying to do so will only lead to frustration or worse consequences. In those cases, we need to adjust our attitude–not our actions. The Advisor, in a positive and reaffirming way, can help the Seeker identify those things which can and cannot be changed. She can focus the conversation on the actions that are needed to make positive changes and on the attitudes surrounding the issue.

Another way to find central themes in advising sessions is to look for causes to the problems being discussed. Particular feelings and habitual reactions are often caused by what is known as a trigger. Certain people, places, or even sounds or smells can activate the recollection of a painful experience in a way that can be almost like reliving that experience over again. All the suffering, emotions, and thoughts about that event will come back again consciously or unconsciously. If those triggers can be identified then the initial problems they caused may also be found. The Advisor can try and work backward historically to try and find that triggering event with questions such as: "When was the first time that you....?" or "When did you begin feeling this way?"

People can also connect painful memories to specific environments and may have to change that environment or situation before any real change can take place.

Exploring Feelings

The Five Primary Emotions

	• _Fear_

Focused on possible pain, suffering, or death

	• _Anger/Resentment_

Motivated by the fight response _Focused on seeking justice against others_

	• _Guilt/Shame_

Motivated by the flight response _Focused on seeking justice against the self_

	• _Anxiety_

Focused on the future

	• _Grief/Depression_

Focused on the past

One of the reasons our challenges in life are so complex is that they usually are entangled in a myriad of emotions. It is not enough to just think through a situation; it is necessary to come to terms with the feelings involved in that situation. It is often not the feelings themselves that cause difficulty as much as it is our inability or unwillingness to face and experience those emotions. In the course of a conversation between an Advisor and a Seeker, the Seeker should be encouraged to discuss and examine any feelings that arise. There are a variety of feelings that can be associated with any situation. Sometimes it becomes necessary to sort out all those individual emotions in order to separate and then look at each.

It can become a challenge for the Seeker to even recognize that a certain feeling exists. If an event has caused the Seeker pain or discomfort, he may have learned how to repress or ignore those painful feelings altogether. The Advisor needs to help the Seeker recognize and identify those feelings. This can be done using the same techniques as discussed in the previous section. The Advisor can paraphrase the Seeker's conversation focusing on any feelings revealed or displayed or she can reflect back particular emotions that are discussed or physically displayed with a statement like "I noticed that you became very upset when you mentioned...." Questions such as: "How did that make you feel?" or "What did that feel like?" help the Seeker identify particular emotions. The Advisor can also share stories in which a particularly related emotion is discussed. The story can even be used to model to the Seeker how to accept and confront the feeling.

It must be remembered that the Seeker, rather than the Advisor, is the authority on his own feelings. Whatever he may be feeling will be genuine and real to him regardless of what the Advisor may think. Treat any feelings that are revealed seriously and with gentle compassion. Whatever feeling he may be experiencing, it is important that the Seeker knows that it is all right to have and express that emotion. Feelings and emotions exist within us for a reason. They are designed to help us prevent harm to ourselves and to overcome difficult changes. Fear and anger are part of the fight or flight response while grief and sorrow come in times of great change or loss. Trying to ignore these feelings or, worse, trying to repress them will only cause further difficulty. On the other hand, trying to force those feelings out of the Seeker may be just as detrimental as ignoring them. The Seeker must be encouraged to deal with painful emotions at his own pace with only slight and gentle urgings from the Advisor.

There are at least five main emotions or pairs of emotions that come up most often in relation to dealing with life challenges each of which should be recognized, identified, and dealt with by the Seeker. They are: fear, anger and resentment, anxiety, grief and depression, and guilt and shame.

Fear is a feeling we get when we believe that we are in danger. Whether that danger is real or imagined, the feeling is real. Fear is part of the flight or fight response that is encoded deep within our brains. If you were to suddenly encounter a large and frightening beast you would be faced with the choice of either trying to fight and defeat it or run from it. Though not all the dangers we face in life are large fang-toothed monsters, the reaction we have to most frightening encounters is the same and it does not matter if the demon we face actually stands before us or only exists in our minds. As we begin to face the choice of fighting or running, our bodies begin to prepare us for the action ahead. Our bodies become filled with adrenaline so that our muscles will have extra strength. The heart rate increases and breathing becomes shallow. We become ready for action. The reaction is the same regardless of the reason.

Dealing With Fear

- *Accept the feeling as real*
- *Determine the cause of the fear*
- *Determine whether the cause of the fear can be harmful or not*
- *Determine whether the cause of the fear can be avoided*

To deal with fear it helps to first accept the feeling as real and serious. The causes of fear are usually persons, places, or events so it often helps to identify the original cause of the fear. Then, determine whether the cause of the fear could truly cause harm or not and whether or not the cause of the fear can be avoided. Each of these will determine the course of action to take. If the originating factor of the fear is truly capable of causing harm and is something, someone, or some place that cannot be avoided in that person's life, then it will be necessary to find some method of protection to defend against that danger. That protection can be a physical act such as learning to defend yourself or seeking a court order or it can be personal act such as learning to love yourself, using positive self-talk, or developing an inner filter to block out harmful words.

If the cause of the fear is not truly harmful and can be avoided, then the Seeker can be encouraged to find ways to stay away from those triggers. If the cause of the fear is not harmful but cannot be avoided, then some type of aversion therapy may be necessary. The goal of this technique is to encourage the fearful person to come in contact with the fear trigger in very small amounts at first while focusing on relaxation techniques and on facing the fear. Over time, the amount of exposure to the trigger is gradually increased until the person becomes comfortable with the encounter.

```
                    ┌──────────────────────┐
                    │   Cause of the Fear  │
                    └──────────────────────┘
              ┌──────────────┴──────────────┐
       ┌─────────────┐              ┌─────────────┐
       │   Harmful   │              │ Not Harmful │
       └─────────────┘              └─────────────┘
       ┌──────┴──────┐                     │
┌─────────────┐ ┌──────────┐      ┌──────────────┐
│Not Avoidable│ │ Avoidable│      │ Not Avoidable│
└─────────────┘ └──────────┘      └──────────────┘
       │             │                     │
┌────────────┐ ┌───────────┐      ┌────────────┐
│ Protection │ │ Avoidance │      │  Aversion  │
│  Methods   │ │Techniques │      │  Therapy   │
└────────────┘ └───────────┘      └────────────┘
```

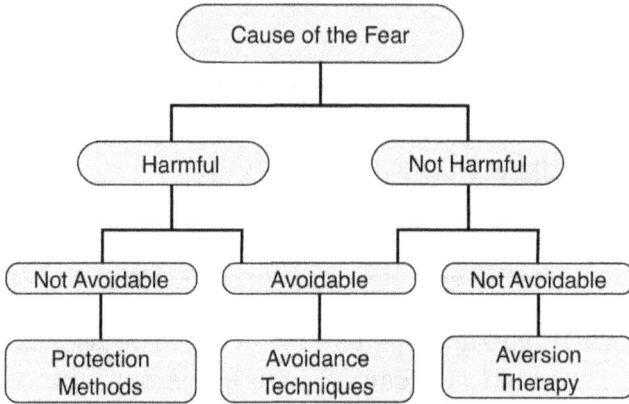

There are two main fears that all people share: the fear of pain and the fear of death. We all try to avoid those things which may cause emotional, mental, or physical pain. Sometimes, however, pain cannot be avoided. In those cases, techniques for dealing with and controlling pain are needed. Meditation techniques can help people learn how to deal with pain. Of course, medication can also help. The fear of death, however, has to be dealt with spiritually. Death is a mystery of life. Having an answer to the question–what happens after we die–is how people come to terms with the reality of death and with the fear associated with it.

Dealing with Anger

- *Accept the feeling as real*
- *Prevent violent action*
- *Redirect the angry energy*
- *Examine expectations and the need to control*
- *Increase tolerance and forgiveness*

If fear is the flight part of the fight-or-flight equation then the choice to fight can result in the emotion of anger. Anger is caused primarily by our need to be in control of ourselves and our environment. We all naturally desire to be loved and accepted by everyone and we all naturally create our own sense of reality. There is nothing inherently wrong with either of these two states of being. At some point in our development as thinking beings, however, we come to realize that neither of these two conditions will be true all the time.

There will be times when we do not love ourselves, when others do not like us, or when things do not go the way we think they should. At this point in development, many individuals begin to develop a level of tolerance for the common mishaps and missteps in life. Those people are able to deal with the stress of not being accepted and not being in control. Events or people that push someone above that level of tolerance, though, are then perceived to be threats and can cause that person to become angry. As with all feelings, there is nothing wrong with being angry. The angry person will feel that he has a right to be angry and the rightness or wrongness of a cause of anger should not be judged by another. The problem with anger is that, if it is not kept under control, it can impede one's ability to think rationally and can cause that person to inflict a violent and harmful action upon another. The need to feel anger needs to be separated from the perceived need to react.

We all have the need to be loved and accepted. When something threatens a positive image of ourselves or our view of the world we can become angry. A child who is ridiculed by others because he is deemed too short or too fat or too ugly, and so on, will come to feel that he is not worthy of the love of others or possibly even of himself. His environment or culture may define what kind of people are acceptable or not acceptable. Young, thin, and tall (the list can go on and on) people may be perceived as more ideal than old, overweight, and short.

Most people accept these socially defined criteria even when they know rationally that such strict parameters in a diverse world are ridiculous. The view others have of us and the view we have of ourselves greatly influences our level of anger and frustration with the world. We can also extend that sense of anger to other people. We can become equally angry when we feel that an injustice is being done to other people. Again, there is nothing wrong with having these angry feelings. In fact, that type of angry concern about an unfair treatment to another can make you want to do something about it. It is how you act on that anger that makes the difference.

We also desire to control our environment; we want to create an image of the world that best suits our own needs and abilities. It is when we expect things to go our own way but they do not that we come face to face with frustration. Frustration takes place when you set up a goal to do something and you fail or are unable to complete that goal. If frustration continues or if we do not accept the disappointing result of our efforts then anger can erupt. The degree of frustration we feel is related to the level of our expectations. When we expect people to act a certain way or things to go a particular way and they do not, we become frustrated; the frustration can lead to anger.

Frustration and anger, when directed toward another person, can lead to further negative emotions such as resentment and blame. When we are not able to control ourselves, others, or our environment, there is a desire not to accept blame for ourselves but to try and blame others instead. Of course, there is truly injustice in the world and there are times when that injustice is caused by others. We are concerned here with the feelings of anger and resentment that can be directed toward others and what those feelings do to the person feeling them. Once again, there is nothing wrong with having those feelings. What is important to consider is how those feelings are affecting the person. Anger and resentment can cloud a person's clear view of a situation or of another person.

In dealing with anger it is important to remember that true anger is a temporary thing. Those who seem to be angry for a long period of time are often using the cloak of anger to hide other things from themselves and/or others. Since anger is part of the fight-or-flight reaction, the body is only able to maintain that state for a short period of time. What seems like long-term anger may initially have been sparked by a trigger event that caused short-term anger but there is something else that is required to sustain those feelings. In long term anger, one learns to play the victim and uses this status as an excuse for not making changes. The cause for the supposed anger is almost always someone else's fault and long-term blame adds to the person's false sense of helplessness.

Short-term anger can be dealt with in other ways. First, as mentioned above, allow the Seeker to accept his anger. Assure him that it is all right to feel angry but it is not all right to act violently upon those feelings. Becoming angry is a way of raising energy in the body. That energy needs to be directed somewhere. If the Seeker knows how to ground, then encourage him to do so. Counting to ten can be a simple method for calming down and re-directing energy. Exercise and sports are other good ways to burn off excess energy. A walk outdoors is usually effective.

The Seeker should be encouraged to listen to his body when he becomes angry so that he can sense the start of angry moments and prevent them from causing a violent reaction. After the initial anger has subsided, it is a good practice to determine the original cause of that anger. What was the angry person trying to control? What were the expectations that were frustrated? Preventing future bouts of anger can be done by re-examining personal expectations and influences. If the Seeker can learn to let go of trying to control all situations and people and if he can increase his personal level of tolerance of others and of the ways of the world then he will come to enjoy life more and become angry less.

Sometimes, though, anger is the appropriate reaction to true injustice. If there is a real threat to your safety then you should act to defend yourself or others. Anger can help to fuel that energy. Having a non-violent reaction to an injustice can let someone know that you will not stand for such abuse or behavior but once the angry reaction has passed it then becomes time to release those feelings and return to a sense of calm and peace.

Sometimes, in order to regain a sense of inner peace, it becomes necessary to forgive others. Forgiveness is never accepting, forgiving, or excusing the harm caused by another and it does not ignore the fact that an injustice has been done. Forgiveness is about releasing the anger directed toward someone so that you can move on in your life.

Dealing with Anxiety

- *Determine the cause of the anxiety*
- *Determine whether or not there is a real threat*
- *Learn relaxation techniques*
- *Find support groups*
- *Connect with spiritual principles*

In a fight-or-flight situation there is yet a third possibility. There are situations in which one cannot run nor engage in battle to ward off a threat. In such a case a person becomes stuck and begins to feel helpless. This feeling brings on a state of anxiety. Having anxiety means to be afraid, nervous, and uncomfortable; it is a confused mixture of both fear and anger. A person in a state of anxiety looks for any way to be relieved of the unending perceived threat. The desire to relieve the constant stress can lead to addictions and neuroses. For example, a person living in a constant fear of becoming sick may take unhealthy amounts of vitamin C and habitually wash his hands several times an hour. For this person, the threat of becoming sick is all consuming because it is perceived to be a danger from which he cannot escape and cannot defeat.

As with fear and anger it is important to help the Seeker identify the cause of the anxiety and determine whether that perceived cause is truly a threat or not. Any causes which can be eliminated or re-framed so that they no longer trigger stress can help the Seeker reduce anxiety. Those stressors which cannot be eliminated will need to be dealt with in a healthy way. The Seeker can be taught to deal with stress by learning relaxation techniques. The Seeker can also be encouraged to find others who have similar difficulties in order to find or develop a support group. Spiritual communities can also be helpful in this regard as long as the members are non-judgmental and supportive (which should be true of any spiritual community).

Advisors can also use examples of nature and spiritual principles to help the Seeker deal with anxiety. All plants and animals go through times of stress brought on by weather, environmental conditions, and the presence of other creatures. Observing the methods of natural things to withstand stress can be a powerful lesson. A few examples: A tree in the midst of a raging storm learns to bend and move without letting go of its roots in the ground. Some animals like penguins learn to withstand months of brutal cold by developing thick coats and banding together. A river overcomes obstacles in its effort to flow to the ocean by very slowly and patiently working its way around them. Sometimes it is helpful to know that no matter how difficult a present situation is, it will inevitably change.

Another common feeling for seekers is grief. This emotion

does not deal with an impending threat; grief comes from the need to overcome a painful loss. Though uncomfortable, grief is a natural process of adjustment. If we are used to having something or someone be an important part of our lives and suddenly that thing or person is gone, we become faced with the reality of living without them. Grief is usually associated with the loss or death of a loved one (more properly called bereavement) but grief can be brought on by any change in life which requires giving up or losing something that has been important. Changing a job, moving to a new location, or even changing an old habit can bring about feelings of grief. All of us grieve to some degree throughout our lives. Grief is a natural reaction and helps bring about the process of dealing with the separation and the need to redefine ourselves.

Signs of Serious Depression
<ul><li>*Drastic changes in eating or sleeping*</li><li>*Drastic changes in overall personality*</li><li>*A loss of interest in normal activities*</li><li>*A sense of worthlessness or hopelessness*</li></ul>

Unfortunately, grief can sometimes lead to depression. Whereas grief aids in adjustment, depression is a debilitating condition that makes it difficult to carry on daily routines and activities. Grief may last anywhere from a few days to several months but depression can linger on for years. Limited Spiritual Advising can be useful to a grieving person but will likely be ineffective for a depressed person. Since depression severely limits a person's ability to cope with normal life and can damage a person's self-image, it can be dangerous and should be treated by a professional. If a Seeker exhibits any of the characteristics listed above and they are obviously interfering in his ability to live a full life, then he should be referred to a healthcare professional.

As always, any discussions of causing harm to the self or to others needs to be reported to authorities and the Seeker should immediately be referred to a professional counselor.

Stages of Grief

- *Denial*
- *Anger*
- *Bargaining*
- *Depression*
- *Acceptance*

The researcher Elizabeth Kubler-Ross has identified five stages that people often encounter when going through a process of grieving or adjusting to a loss. It is important to remember that not everyone goes through all these stages nor do all people go through them in order. Also, it is not necessary for one to go through one stage before being able to go on to another. A person can begin at the first stage and move immediately on the final stage depending on their ability to cope and adjust. Some might reach the fourth stage but then need to begin again at the first. There is no set format for dealing with grief and a person will deal with it in his or her own way but knowing these five stages can help the Advisor recognize the part of the process a grieving person may be going through.

When first being faced with a difficult loss, a person may deny the reality of the change being forced upon them. Making changes is difficult and we often try to resist or deny painful changes. When we lose something or someone upon which we depend in our lives our minds are, at first, unable to comprehend that reality. We may become numb in an effort to resist the need to experience the pain of loss. We reject the idea that we must now re-align ourselves to a new reality. We may, at first, be unable to react at all. When we do respond, our bodies may react violently and we may try to actually fight the reality of the new situation. We can become angry and turn our response outward or we may turn inward and feel guilty believing that we may have caused the original event. When the reality of the situation begins to truly settle in, we may then begin to try and regain what was lost. Some people will try to bargain with a deity–pleading with him or her to change the situation. Some may search for an immediate replacement (sometimes referred to as "being on the rebound") or a close substitute.

If the person can finally realize that the loss is a permanent reality that cannot be replaced or denied, then a state of profound sadness can set in. Though Kubler-Ross uses the term depression, that word has come to have a clinical meaning as discussed in the previous paragraph. I prefer to use the term intense sadness. One who experiences intense sadness may cry and feel distraught but will be closer to the final stage of acceptance. In the stage of intense sadness, the person will realize the need to integrate the loss and redefine his life but will not be quite ready to do so. Only in the final stage–acceptance–will he finally be able to make the necessary changes to his life.

People who experience grief mostly need someone to listen to them. Never should a person be told to just "get over it and move on." Unfortunately, this is often the message of societies that shy away from experiencing emotions. To truly overcome a difficult loss it is necessary to go through the grieving process. Grief often comes in waves as the whole person makes gradual adjustments. Thus, a person may seem to be better only to grieve again later. Usually subsequent bouts of grief lessen in intensity with each occurrence (whereas a depressed person will experience recurring bouts at similar levels). It is good for a Seeker to know this concept so that he can accept any feelings of grief that may return.

To deal with grief, the Seeker should learn to accept the loss by going through one or all of the stages of grief. Next, it will be important to reduce the strength of the feeling attached to the lost person or thing. This does not mean that there should be no residual feelings at all but the emotions that make the Seeker feel the need to have that thing in his life will need to be released. The loss that has been experienced will naturally leave the Seeker feeling that there is a gap in his life. Though this gap can never be adequately filled nor should the Seeker try to completely replace the loss, he should be encouraged to find other people or develop new habits that can enrich his life.

If the grief is due to a loss of life, then the Seeker will need to come to terms with his understanding of death. No one knows what happens after death which makes it a topic for faith and spirituality. The Advisor should work with the Seeker to explore his view while the Advisor should only offer her own view when it may be helpful. If the Seeker's view of death is not a comforting one then it may need to be examined or alternative views may need to be offered.

Techniques for Guilt and Shame
• *Identify the source of the feelings* • *Examine the ethical assumptions* • *Make amends* • *Forgive yourself* • *Change the perception*

Feelings of guilt and shame come from our image of ourselves and our perception of what is right and wrong. Both are inner punishments based on personal ethics and a view of how we believe that we should act and live. Guilt is experienced when a person perceives that an action is deemed wrong while shame is the feeling that a person is not good or is not worthy of the affections of others. Neither feeling is necessarily inappropriate in small doses and can help a person regulate his own behavior but when the person has a rigid set of personal ethics or a poor self image, feelings of guilt or shame can be frequent and debilitating.

To overcome guilt and shame the Seeker must examine the cause of the guilt and view it in light of his overall view of right action and self-image. Have the Seeker take a close look at his personal or assumed ethical principles to see which one led to the feelings of guilt or shame. If an action was taken that is viewed as inappropriate then something should be done to apologize and/or make the situation right (if possible). Once restitution has taken place, the Seeker should be encouraged to forgive himself and not allow that action to color his view of himself. Finally, the Seeker's view of right and wrong and of himself may need to be examined and he should be encouraged to make adjustments to those beliefs if they are overly negative or crippling. The judgement of the appropriateness of an act can be separated from the judgment of the value of the self.

Exploring The Spiritual Connection

After the Seeker has defined his problem or problems and has revealed and examined his feelings concerning those issues, it is important that the Spiritual Advisor help him reveal and explore his spiritual connection.

The Spiritual Connection
<ul><li>*Define core values*</li><li>*Define concrete actions*</li></ul>

Although it is possible to have an advising session without discussing spirituality at all, advising is more powerful and meaningful when it is connected to a person's spirituality. Understanding a person's spiritual perspective helps you to understand his view of life and his relationship to the universe and it helps you look for clues and tools that can be applied when dealing with the Seeker's challenges. Spiritual practices can be used for exploring and dealing with difficult problems. When you see spirituality as the way in which we connect to ourselves, to others, to Earth, and to the universe, then it is easy to see how daily problems may be approached through a spiritual outlook. It is important to remember that even if the Advisor and the Seeker are in the same spiritual tradition, they may each view things differently.

The Big Questions

- *What is the ultimate reality of all things?*
- *What is your relationship to that reality?*
- *What is your role in life?*
- *What is death and how does it affect you now?*

Begin exploring the Seeker's spiritual outlook by asking him about his core values with questions about his belief in the ultimate reality of the universe, his role in that reality, how he hopes to live his life based on that reality, and what is his understanding of death

These are big questions to be sure and the Seeker may not even have answers for them but thinking about these things will ultimately color his view on everything else in his life. The point of such a conversation in the context of Spiritual Advising is not to completely flesh out answers to all these questions. That type of intense spiritual exploration is better done through the practice of Spiritual Direction. Instead, the purpose of the discussion should be to help the Advisor find things that may be useful in helping the Seeker find solutions to his problems. Pay special attention to any positive and affirming things that may come up in the discussion. Listen for how the Seeker finds connections and what gives him energy and purpose. Look for anything that may be a possible strength to use in searching for answers and positive directions.

Defining Concrete Actions

The final step in the process of Spiritual Advising is to define some concrete actions for the Seeker to take to help him overcome his challenges. To do this, decide what type of actions or exercises might be useful and then assign specific exercises or homework. A follow-up session should then be planned. To determine what actions might be helpful for the Seeker, it is important to pay attention to his discussions to find anything that might indicate a strength or exception to the problem. You might also ask the Seeker about such times with questions like: "Were there any times when you were not feeling this way?" or "When do you most feel happy?" or you can ask him to imagine positive actions by asking questions like: "What would it be like if you did not have this problem?" or "If you could do something to make it all go away what would your life look like?" You can also listen for subtle clues from the Seeker himself. Often times we know deep down what we need to do to overcome a challenge though we may not want to admit it. Those answers can be revealed through words or actions by the Seeker. One of the easiest ways to discover some actions to help the Seeker, however, is to ask the Seeker himself. There are times when the Seeker knows exactly what it is that he needs to do to solve a problem but simply needs encouragement and support from you to take those steps.

Determining Concrete Action
- *Define specific goals*
- *Seek a single outcome*
- *Negotiate, not dictate*
- *Assign exercises or homework*
- *Follow up on progress*
- *Assess progress against goals*
- *Begin the process again until goals are met*

To establish concrete actions to take, define some limited and practical goals, assign some homework to accomplish those goals, create a contract between yourself and the Seeker, and define some way to assess the work being done. Goals set for the Seeker need to be small, specific, and focused on a possible solution to a problem. Small and simple goals are easier to obtain than large and lofty ones. A task which adds new possibilities to life is usually easier and likely to be more successful than one that seeks to eliminate something. Though small goals may be part of a larger goal, it is important for the Seeker to be able to succeed with the use of small and easy steps.

The completion of even a ridiculously simple task can be very meaningful to the Seeker. It empowers him and lets him know that he is capable of success. The goal should be focused on a single outcome that will help in some small way to overcome a challenge. The goal should be centered on a specific task assigned as homework. Either in verbal or written form, you and the Seeker should agree on an appropriate plan of action. It is best not to try and dictate to the Seeker what you think should be done but that both of you negotiate the task. The Seeker should feel like the task is as much his idea as it was yours so that he can take ownership of it. Part of that negotiation is to agree upon a way to assess the task. What will represent success at its completion? A follow-up meeting should be planned to discuss the task and its effectiveness. Depending on the progress, the process of determining concrete actions should begin again with re-defined goals until the overall goal of wholeness is closer to reality.

There are many activities that can be assigned as homework that can help the Seeker improve his situation. Many of them will be similar to spiritual practices and this is no accident. Good spiritual practices bring positive effects to your life and they can be used to overcome difficult challenges. There are many spiritual practices that can be helpful as assignments for healing but Advisors also need to be creative in coming up with appropriate actions in unique circumstances.

Spiritual Practices for Assignments

- *letter writing*
- *prayer*
- *meditation*
- *seeking forgiveness*
- *making amends*
- *visualization*
- *affirmation*
- *journaling*
- *witnessing*
- *ritual*

If a Seeker has a difficulty in not being able to express himself, then **Writing a Letter** can be a powerful technique. The letter might never be sent to the recipient and that does not matter. What is important is that the Seeker take time to carefully plan out and write down what he wants to say without restrictions. The letter should be reviewed and revised until it actually reflects the feelings that need to be expressed. The letter can then be sent, saved in a special place, or burned as part of a release. Before actually sending any such letters, however, a discussion about the possible consequences should take place.

Similar to letter writing, the practice of **Prayer** can be a good way to express feelings. Prayers can be spoken aloud and addressed to a deity, or to the spirit of life, or to the life energy of another. Prayers can be used to reveal inner feelings, ask for forgiveness, ask for other needs, or to be thankful.
Meditation is another powerful technique that can be used for inner exploration and to develop states of relaxation and inner peace. For those who feel they have acted wrongly toward another, the practice of seeking forgiveness and making amends–if done with good and true intentions–can help them find inner peace. Visualization of how the Seeker can act in specific situations can become a way to develop new habits and attitudes in the mind before actually trying to do so in real situations.

Another way to change attitudes and habits or to act as a reminder of specific goals is to use **Affirmations** or short positive or motivational statements that are repeated at least once a day. Affirmations are often done with the Seeker speaking into a mirror so that he is talking directly to himself.

Journaling is another way for the Seeker to express his feelings to himself and to record his progress during the day. Journaling can be an important tool for helping to identify triggers and other causes of stress and difficulty. Some people document their lives in scrapbooks or photo albums.

Witnessing is a practice in which the Seeker imagines that he has a higher self that can be a separate entity and that stands aside from him. The witness lovingly, patiently, and without judgment observes what happens throughout the day. This witness is able to report things as they truly are without the bias of the individual Seeker. In time, the Seeker can learn to develop this witness and actually be able to use it for seeing situations more clearly.

Finally, **Ritual** can be a powerful tool for overcoming challenges. Ritual is a way of elevating simple actions until they have special meaning. Ritual done regularly can add a sense of predictability and control in a chaotic life.

Follow-Up
• _Review progress_ • _Offer praise for success_ • _Consider future action_

Once a plan of action has been determined, it is important to also come up with a follow-up plan. Plan ahead for at least one more meeting in which you and the Seeker can discuss the effectiveness of the activity. Discuss how you will determine whether or not the goal was reached and how successful it was in helping the Seeker overcome his challenge. Plan for success as much as possible but assure the Seeker that not completely meeting the goal does not make the Seeker a failure–separate the act from the actor. Make sure you find some kind of success–no matter how small–in what the Seeker has attempted and offer praise for that success.

When you next meet, determine whether or not the Seeker was successful. Look for anything that might be considered a positive improvement even if the stated goal was not fully met. If you determine that the Seeker was successful then it is time to bring the Seeker/Advisor relationship to an end.

Reasons for Referral

- *The Seeker expresses a desire to harm himself*
- *The Seeker expresses a desire to harm others*
- *The Seeker makes no significant change after three meetings*
- *The Seeker or the Advisor cross personal boundaries of separation*
- *The Seeker no longer feels comfortable with the situation*
- *The Advisor no longer feels comfortable with the situation*
- *The Advisor feels she can be of no further help*

If the Seeker was not totally successful, then the Advisor will need to decide if some more sessions might be helpful or if referral is necessary. You should consider referral if nothing seems to be helping or if either the Seeker or Advisor no longer wish to continue for any reason.

Remember that spiritual advising is a short-term and temporary non-professional activity and should be limited to three to five sessions with one person. Be as honest and as frank with yourself as you are with the Seeker. If you are unable to help the Seeker find a solution to his problems it may be necessary to refer him to someone else. Be ready with names and phone numbers of caring professionals in your area. (A list of suggested people and a place to record their information is provided in the appendix of this section.) If you decide to try again, then it may be helpful to know some of the common reasons for not meeting advising goals.

Resistance Or Failure

There are many reasons why a Seeker may not meet the goals that both you and he has agreed upon. It may at first seem odd that someone would come to you for help and then be unwilling or unable to make changes for his own good. The reasons for this are often based on the fact that we all have conflicting needs and desires within ourselves, that we all have certain levels of abilities and limitations, and that we all naturally resist change.

Forces of Influence
<ul><li>*Agency*</li><li>*Communion*</li><li>*Security*</li></ul>

All humans are pulled upon by the opposing forces of agency and communion. The force of agency creates in us the desire to be an individual. All people seek to establish some independence. We seek to separate ourselves from others and create our own legacy. This is the force that causes us to try different things, to travel, or to create new things. The force of communion is the desire to be loved and accepted by others. We all desire to be part of something else and to love and be loved by others. This is the force that calls us to seek interest groups, find a mate and start a family, or to follow certain trends.

We are also influenced by a need for security. This manifests in our desire to be safe and comfortable. We all wish to have some consistency or routine in our lives. We all wish to live in a safe place and be able to take care of our basic needs. This is the force that resists change, develops routines and habits, or causes us to "nest." It is because we all have these various forces within us that we may act in conflicting ways. An outward desire to change (agency) may conflict with an inward desire to maintain a routine (security) even if that routine is not healthy and it may also conflict with a desire not to seem weird or different to friends (communion). The intersection of these needs causes confusion especially if the person is not aware of them. All these needs must be addressed jointly in order to encourage change. When they are not, there will be resistance by the Seeker which may be either conscious or unconscious.

It is possible that even after seeing through the confusion of conflicting forces and identifying the changes that need to be made that the Seeker is simply unable to make those changes. The deeper a habit is grafted onto a person's identity and core personality the more difficult it is to change that habit. We are all born with certain strengths and weaknesses. Weakness can be worked upon and strengths can be used to overcome weaknesses but both will always be present, to some degree. Part of the process of healthy growing is in learning to identify and work with those strengths and weaknesses. Trying to do something and then learning that it cannot be done is not really a failure if something is learned in the process. If a complementary strength can be identified then an alternative plan may be possible.

What may at first seem impossible in many cases is not really impossible; it may be simply that the Seeker is trying to avoid making a change. Unconsciously or consciously the Seeker will put up some kind of resistance to the change and to anyone trying to encourage him to change. It is hoped that in the process of Spiritual Advising the Advisor and the Seeker have discussed or discovered a need for some change which can help the Seeker overcome his challenge. It does not matter if that realization is vaguely or fully realized in order for resistance to arise. Chances are it will not be the first time that the resistance to this change has come up. The resistance will be fueled primarily by a fear of change.

The Fear of Change

- *It may be too much work*
- *It may require a revision of self-identity*
- *It may require a change in habits*

Change can be challenging in and of itself. Change of habit or of the personality usually requires hard work since we may become used to doing things or acting in a certain way. Change in personality requires us to redefine ourselves and change in habits require us to redefine our lives. Both of these things can be frightening and even painful. It takes a certain degree of courage and fortitude to be willing to take on such changes and it is natural to be resistant to them.

Resistance to Change

- *Ignoring or denying the problem (repression)*
- *Blaming the problem on someone else (transference)*
- *Not taking responsibility for the change (rationalization)*

One of the most common and easiest ways to resist change is to simply deny that the problem actually exists but repressed problems can be ignored for only a limited time. At some point, there will be a consequence to burying the problem. Denial can take place by trying to completely ignore the problem and also repress any feelings associated with it. With repression, feelings are buried deep within the psyche and people will do anything to avoid those feelings or any connection to them.

One way to avoid difficult feelings and underlying problems is to put blame on another person or to see a helping person as an image of authority from childhood. This is known as transference. Through transference a person literally transfers feelings from within himself to another person. It is easy to blame someone else for our own mistakes and inadequacies but we are responsible for our own choices and actions in life. People who cannot take on that responsibility will look for others to take on the burden.

People with unresolved issues may see others around them as characters in a never-ending tragedy rather than as separate and unique individuals. The characters of this tragedy can be anyone–this will be especially true for people who may be in positions of power and authority such as a Spiritual Advisor. When this happens, the Seeker may see the Advisor as a childhood authority figure and place upon her all the problems and challenges he faced with that individual. Often that leads to intense and inappropriate behavior.

A third way to avoid difficult feelings and problems is to rationalize them away. The Seeker will try to justify what he thinks are perfectly valid reasons for not dealing with the problem. Sometimes the Seeker will find reasons why the change is not needed. No matter how unreasonable the justification may seem to you, the Seeker will have convinced himself of the validity of his judgment. He may have even developed or found ways to reinforce his patterns of avoidance.

For example, a person may have learned as a child that he gets more attention from his parents when he is feeling ill and may have been ignored when he was healthy. As he grows up, he associates sickness with getting caring and attention so he develops patterns of becoming or thinking that he is often sick. Though he may not actually enjoy being sick, he will look for the attention he think he deserves when he is sick by constantly seeing a doctor or another professional helper. He will justify to himself that he really cannot help being sick and, therefore, needs to see someone often. The same pattern can take place in an advising situation where Seekers come to an Advisor not so much to get better but to seek something else that they once received or desired from childhood authority figures. People can even justify their actions by believing that they are not truly worth being any better. This is, of course, a self-esteem issue but it can lead to a type of negative rationalization.

Any reason for resistance can be a difficult thing to change because the Seeker will have developed defenses and methods for not looking at the core problem and trying to force him to do so may only lead to a further avoidance of the problem. The Seeker can only be encouraged to be open and honest with himself so that he can slowly begin to face his problems head on. The Advisor can offer a supportive, caring, and safe environment for him to do so but should also be aware that resistance can be a warning about deeply buried issues. Such issues may take a long time with a trained professional to uncover and it may be best to seek a referral in such cases.

Signs of Resistance

- *Consistently unproductive discussions*
- *Unusual or inappropriate behaviors*
- *Avoidance*

There are several signs that can be used to predict the presence of resistance. Discussions with the Seeker may be completely unproductive. There may be moments of silence that do not move the conversation forward. We have discussed how silence can actually be a useful tool in Sacred Listening but it can also be a sign that the Seeker is unable to put some feeling or thought into words. The Seeker can also stall the conversation through excessive talking, laughing, or joking which manages to fill the time that you have with him but helps him avoid any serious conversation. The Seeker can use inappropriate behavior to avoid a frank discussion; he may cause a scene or act out. The Seeker can suddenly become overly friendly or even seductive in order to distract your attention from the point of discussion.

On the opposite side of the spectrum, he may suddenly become completely withdrawn. If the conversation goes well, the Seeker may still demonstrate signs of resistance by not completing assignments he has agreed to do. He might be excessively late or absent from planned meetings with you or other helpers. He may stop doing his spiritual practice or try to avoid any people or places that remind him of his problem. All of these can be clues to the fact that the Seeker is trying to avoid something from within himself. It is important for you to encourage him to see if he is avoiding something. Only by facing the truth will he be free of the problem he is resisting.

Reasons for Possible Failure by the Advisor

- *Not accepting limitations*
- *Ambiguity*
- *Trying to be the savior*
- *Frustration*
- *Unsolved personal issues*
- *Counter-transference*

So far, we have examined reasons for possible failure caused by the Seeker but an unsuccessful session may be the result of shortcomings of the Advisor as well. If you find yourself having difficulty responding to the Seeker, saying things you are not really sure about, constantly changing your posture, or having difficulty paying attention to the Seeker, then you may be encountering your own resistance.

Sometimes an Advisor may resist the fact that she might not be able to help everyone. That which you have asked your Seeker to do, so you must do yourself. Accept your own limitations, be clear, accept the lead of your Seeker, stay centered, and be honest with yourself. All Advisors are human beings with limitations and personal conflicts. Understand that you will not be able to help everyone. Learn from your mistakes as a natural part of growth and become a better Advisor. Be clear about who you are and what you want to do in the session with your Seeker. Remind yourself that advising is a spiritual act that can be challenging and taxing. You will need to constantly draw in energy to stay centered and focused. An advising session is a lot like doing an active meditation such as Tai Chi or Yoga: you need to focus on the movements–but stay centered. Try not to be a rescuer or a savior.

Your job is not to save anyone. Your job is to give room and encouragement for the Seeker to find his own solution. Try not to offer an answer–even if it seems like the most obvious solution to you. Remain true to yourself and your own feelings. You are not a robot without feelings or opinions; it is by being a feeling person that you learn to be a caring Advisor. If you find that certain feelings or intrusive thoughts arise while you are listening, then pay attention to them. You may have your own issues to resolve that are brought to the surface by the words of your Seeker. Most Advisors also seek advising for the practice of being on the other side of the discussion and to resolve those very issues that arise. Learn to let go of any frustrations or other energies that may arise and get in the way of the conversation.

If you catch yourself engaging in inappropriate behavior, becoming punitive to your Seeker, or constantly resorting to lecturing and preaching, you may be experiencing countertransference. A problem arises for an Advisor when she projects feelings or models of behavior upon her Seeker. When a Seeker projects onto an Advisor it is called transference. When an Advisor does the same or projects back onto the Seeker it is called countertransference. The causes of countertransference can be plentiful and quite complex. Sometimes the advisor desires to be admired and loved by the Seeker.

It is easy to be swept away by the feelings of dominance and authority in an advising relationship. The Seeker will come to depend on the Advisor for acceptance and approval. He will come to value what she says and respect her for her willingness to help. He may transfer upon her images of a caring and loving parent or the role of other figures in his life such as close friends and lovers. She will be unconsciously invited to take that role and then transfer upon the Seeker her own roles and images. We all desire affection and acceptance but the advising role is not the appropriate place for such needs. There must be a very clear role for the Advisor in any session. All advising situations require some bit of professional distance. Even if Seeker and Advisor are close friends before advising begins, it must be understood that the relationship will change during a session for the benefit of both individuals.

Exercises

Solo Exercises

Solo Exercise no. 1 - Advising Techniques

Review a personal situation and break it down with advising techniques:

1. Define the problem.
2. Explore your feelings related to it.
3. Relate it to your own spiritual connection.

Solo Exercise no. 2 - Personal Feelings

Explore your own personal feelings.

1. What causes you the greatest fear?
2. What causes you the greatest anger?

3. What causes you the greatest anxiety?

4. What causes you the greatest grief?

5. What causes you the greatest guilt?

✻

Solo Exercise no. 3 - Controlling Anger

1. Review what causes you anger.

2. Concentrate on that experience then practice calming yourself.

✻

Solo Exercise no. 4 - Controlling Fear

1. Review what causes you fear.

2. Concentrate on that experience then practice calming yourself.

✻

Solo Exercise no. 5 - Explore Core Spiritual Values

1. What do you believe is the ultimate reality of the universe?

2. What is your role in that reality?

3. How do you live your life based on that reality?

4. What is your understanding of death and how does it affect your life now?

✻

Solo Exercise no. 6 - Letter Writing

1. Write a letter to someone expressing inner feelings.

2.
   Either send or burn it.

Partner Exercises

Partner Exercise no. 1 - Paraphrasing

The object of this exercise is to listen for key words to use to paraphrase what the Seeker is saying to you. Have one person read a very short story while the other person listens for specific people, places, or emotions. When one of these is encountered the listener will paraphrase what has been said back to the reader. The reader will check to see if the paraphrase is accurate. The paraphraser can use an opening statement such as "What I hear you saying is...." or "It sounds to me like you are saying...." etc.

❋

Partner Exercise no. 2 - Asking Questions

This exercise is to help you learn how to ask helpful and open-ended questions. As before, have a partner read a story or discuss an event. The listener will listen and ask questions about what the storyteller is revealing. Remember to use open-ended questions that help to further the story. Do not insist on answers. Let the the storyteller lead at all times. The storyteller should listen to the questions and evaluate their effectiveness in encouraging him or her to keep the story moving.

❋

Partner Exercise no. 3 - Identifying Control

It is important to help a Seeker identify things that truly can or cannot be changed in a situation. Have a partner describe a situation or story from his or her past. The listener should then ask the storyteller what within the story are things that could have been changed and what were not.

❈

Partner Exercise no. 4 - Identifying the Core Emotion

It is often difficult to find a core emotion when a Seeker is experiencing a variety of emotions. This exercise is designed to help practice getting to that core emotion. Have the partner describe a confusing and emotional situation (real or not). The listener should pay attention to cue words describing emotions and ask questions about feelings. Questions such as "How did that make you feel?" help to encourage the exploration of feelings. The listener should try to find a single emotion that underlies the other emotions discussed. As always, let the storyteller lead the discussion and do not try to force an answer.

❈

Partner Exercise no. 5 - Dealing With Fear

Everyone deals with fear in their lives–it is unavoidable–but we can learn to cope with it. Have your partner describe a real or imaginary fearful situation. Using the section on determining concrete goals, define a plan of action to overcome the fear: define a simple and attainable goal, assign homework using one of the helpful techniques discussed in this chapter (or a similar technique), create a contract, and discuss ways of gauging success.

❈

Partner Exercise no. 6 - Dealing With Anger

Anger and fear are two sides of a feeling of being out of control with your environment. To overcome those feelings, it can be helpful to reframe the situation that caused them. Have your partner discuss a real or imagined time when he or she was angry. Ask your partner to go through the process of dealing with anger: accept the anger, prevent violent action, redirect the energy, examine expectations and the need to control, and increase tolerance. Be sure to examine the underlying attitudes behind the initial anger. Using the section on determining concrete goals, define a plan of action to overcome the anger.

❈

Partner Exercise no. 7 - Dealing With Grief

Grief is yet another unavoidable emotion in life. Have your partner discuss a real or imagined time when he or she lost someone close. Have the storyteller discuss going through each of the five stages of grief: denial, anger, bargaining, sadness and acceptance. Next, discuss how the storyteller can learn to overcome the grief through the three steps to overcoming grief: accept the loss, surrender the emotional connection, and develop new relationships and habits. Using the section on determining concrete goals and define a plan of action to overcome the grief.

❈

Partner Exercise no. 8 - Dealing With Guilt

Feelings of guilt are dependent upon a person's sense of personal ethics. Have your partner discuss a real or imagined time when he or she felt guilty or ashamed of something. Go through the steps of relieving guilt: identify the source, examine the ethical assumptions, make amends, forgive yourself, and change perception. Using the section on determining concrete goals and define a plan of action to overcome the guilt.

❈

Partner Exercise no. 9 - Exploring the Spiritual Connection

Have your partner explain his or her spiritual principles based on the following four questions: what do you believe is the ultimate reality of the universe, what do you believe is your part to play in the universe, how do you decide to live out your life based on these first two principles, and what do you believe happens at the end of life? Examine the answers to each of these as much as your partner is comfortable doing. Look for things in the belief system that can be used as strengths to help him or her get through difficult life challenges and situations.

�֎

Partner Exercise no. 10 - Using Sources

Different sources of inspiration can help people better understand their situations and challenges. These sources include books of wisdom, myths, teachings from wise people, the observation of nature, and trusting sources from within. Read a myth, story, or other source of wisdom to your partner. Discuss the themes of the source and how that source can be used to help others. If either of you discover sources that may be useful in sessions, be sure to write them down for future reference.

✖

Partner Exercise no. 11 - Observing the Pull of Agency and Communion

Have your partner discuss a real or imagined situation. Discuss the parts of the story that revealed a desire to expand the self through assertion and self-expression (agency). Discuss the parts of the story that revealed a desire to be a part of something or to be with others through connection and association (communion). Discuss the parts of the story where a resistance to any change took place (security). Finally, discuss the possible interaction of these forces.

❋

<u>Partner Exercise no. 12 - Reframing and Choices</u>

Many situations can become less stressful and challenging if they can be viewed in another light and if the Seeker can remember that he has the ability to choose his reactions to all situations. Have your partner discuss a real or imagined situation and then discuss how the situation could be reframed to find any positive or alternative views. Discuss the original reactions to the situation and observe if the storyteller could have chosen to react in any other way that would have been more helpful.

Special Advising Situations

It is not possible to cover in a single book all the possible advising and counseling situations that a Spiritual Advisor may encounter but there are a few special situations that bear mention. This section will provide a starting point for helping advise people who are dying or dealing with death, people who encounter frightening spiritual situations (a spiritual emergency), people in immediate crisis, and individuals contemplating suicide. Each of these provide unique challenges for the Advisor. As with all subjects in this book, be honest about your experience and ability with your Seeker and be willing to learn as much as you can. Many of these situations require a referral or additional people to help out. Spiritual Advisors are not professionals nor should they act as such. You may the first person to be asked to help but you should not be the only one. In cases like these, the Advisor will be more like a triage nurse who enters a battlefield. You can offer aid and comfort and, in some cases, can help bandage some wounds, but serious repair work must be done by a professional.

Care For The Dying

Being with a dying person can be a particularly tough challenge for any person and that includes Spiritual Advisors.

Care for the Dying

- *Help them through the grief process*
- *Encourage a progression of feelings*
- *Help them choose their preparations*

Our society does not like to talk about death and much of the culture pretends as if death is not even real. To be comfortable in being with the dying you must also be comfortable with the thought of death itself. Death is a part of life. If you can come to grips with the reality and inevitability of your own death then you will be able to help another person experience those same fears. Make it part of your spiritual practice to face the reality of death and let it teach you about life rather than fear it.

People are born with a desire to survive. It only makes sense that, as living beings, we wish to continue for as long as health and conditions allow. In order to grow and experience, we must strive to remain alive. It is only natural, then, for someone who has learned that she is going to die to be resistant to that reality. Regardless of what any spiritual teacher or book of wisdom may say, no one knows what really happens after death and facing this reality can be very frightening. But, it can be helpful to at least have some theories about death. These are often defined by spiritual traditions.

People who are dying want to be treated just as other living people are treated–with dignity and respect. They want to feel alive as long as they can. Mostly, they will need to talk and express their feelings to someone they think is going to actually listen to them. They do not need lectures, life lessons, or sermons about the preciousness of life. What they mostly want is someone to be genuinely present with them; they want a Sacred Listener. They may, at first, speak in stories or symbols as they come to grips with the terms of their own death. Any manner in which he or she wants to communicate should be encouraged even if that manner is sitting in silent embrace. What a dying person says and does will depend on the particular stage of death acceptance she is experiencing.

We grieve the same whether it is for ourselves or for others. At first, the dying person will not be able to accept the truth of his own death. At this stage it is important to let him come to his own realization and not try to force him beyond that. When he does come to understand the reality of his situation he may then become angry at the world or at some spiritual concept. He may come to look for something or someone to blame. If he can get through the anger, he may come to try and bargain with the universe to let him live. When both the anger and deal-making subsides, he may then become depressed. Finally, some people are able to get through all these experiences and be able to accept the reality of the situation. Like all stages, every person experiences them differently and sometimes only some, not all, stages are experienced. A person with a strong spirituality and positive outlook toward death is more likely to reach a state of acceptance sooner than someone who is fearful of death.

There are certain things that will become very important to the dying person and they may be things with which you can offer help. First of all, the person will need to do the personal grief work mentioned above. He will need strength, encouragement, and a strong presence from someone who can let him progress through his feelings. It will be helpful if he has a strong supportive community such as a spiritual group that can take turns being with him and helping him with his needs. He may have some unfinished issues with people in his life that he may want to work through. The dying often need to find a way to express some very personal thoughts and feelings and may need assistance in finding ways to do this. The dying person may question his faith and its teachings about death. The Advisor will need to be able to provide some possibilities and be ready to face some tough questions. The Seeker may need help in exploring his own answers.

Most dying people wish to die at home with family and friends at their side but this is not always possible. Listen to his requests and do your best to fulfill them. Ask if he would desire any specific rituals either before or after her death (questions like this need to be asked only after the grief work has been done) and do your best to see that all around him treat him with the same dignity and respect demanded of you. People that surround the dying will also be dealing with their own levels of grief and will be struggling with their conflicting feelings about death. Being with the dying can force people to face that which they may have been trying to ignore all their lives. An Advisor may be called upon to help more than just the dying person.

Crisis

There are times when you may be called upon to help someone in a crisis situation. This type of situation is different from a typical advising session. In a crisis, there exists a real and immediate threat to a person's safety. Attention to the victim (or victims) of a crisis is needed during or soon after the crisis occurs. During this time, the victim of a crisis will be in a confused and panicked state but will, very likely, be willing to be helped. The first goal for any Advisor in a crisis situation is to see that the victim is safe. Any help that needs to be called should be done immediately. After seeking safety, subsequent advising should help the person calm down to regain a sense of control.

A crisis does not necessarily have to come in the face of a physical danger. Someone can feel in crisis if he encounters a situation that he cannot handle effectively. When a person's standard methods of problem solving and coping are pushed beyond their limits, a sense of dire panic can ensue. This creates a crisis situation. Any life challenge can bring upon a crisis stage: death, severe illness, birth, changes in relationships, violence, disruptions in routines, or any personal or communal disaster. All these, of course, are subjects that are common to the ears of any spiritual advisor and are not by themselves reasons for crisis. Crisis is reached when the Seeker is not emotionally equipped to deal with the sudden and devastating change that a crisis brings into a life.

Even though disaster and danger often comes on quickly, there are actually several stages of crisis. If it is possible to recognize these as they occur, then intervention may be possible and the final stage of the process may be avoided.

Stages of Crisis
<ul><li>*Threat*</li><li>*Breakdown of Coping Skills*</li><li>*Panic*</li><li>*Disorganization*</li></ul>

In the beginning of a crisis situation there is a threat to the safety, health, and/or welfare of the person or group. This threat can be physical, mental, emotional, or spiritual (more on that in the next section). People deal with minor threats on a daily basis and we have all developed coping techniques to overcome or avoid those threats but, sometimes, a threat can come on so strong that typical coping responses are too weak, too late, or too ineffective to help. At this stage, those coping techniques break down as does a person's sense of control and security. This is when panic sets in. Without finding a way to cope with this panic, a person will enter the fourth stage of crisis where the organization of the personality begins to fall apart. There will be a disconnect to the self as the body goes into a kind of shock and the mind begins to shut down. In some cases a person can have lasting psychological trauma from having experienced a personality disorganization.

Crisis Steps
<ul><li>*Get the person out of danger*</li><li>*Define the threat*</li><li>*Find ways to seek help*</li></ul>

A Spiritual Advisor or any type of person who can help in a crisis situation should first seek to keep the person in crisis out of danger–whatever that danger may be perceived to be. Once safety has been ensured, try to define the threat that caused the crisis. Offer assistance by being calm, supportive, and non-judgmental. Be respectful and accepting of the person and her situation. Try to explore with him some alternatives for the immediate situation and then make plans to pursue those alternatives. When you have devised a plan, make sure that he clearly understands the plan and then follow-through to see he has enacted the plan. In the aftermath of the crisis there is usually a wide span of difficult emotions that are experienced and advising sessions or referrals to other helping professionals will probably be needed. As an Advisor, you can encourage the victim to seek out these avenues of help.

Spiritual Emergency

The spiritual emergency is a unique crisis situation that, more than any other, needs the services of a Spiritual Advisor. There are times when a person can be overwhelmed by a spiritual experience. If that encounter with spiritual reality is not one that a person is prepared to face, a sense of dread and fear can overtake that person. The purpose of many spiritual practices is to get the Seeker to break away from a standard set of conventions and move toward a connection with the universal. This can be like the moment you first look over the edge of the Grand Canyon or stare into the dark night sky and realize you are but a small part of the cosmos. More daunting can be the realization that you are intimately connected with this vast universe. In such a moment one can feel lost and disoriented or can even feel completely disconnected. A sense of sudden panic may take over which can be as emotionally real as a heart attack.

Steps for Spiritual Emergencies

- *Calm the person down*
- *Listen*
- *Review the experience for spiritual lessons*
- *Try to incorporate the lessons learned*

If you find that your Seeker is beginning to enter into a desperate panicked state, the first thing to do is to try and calm him down. Simply reassure him that he is all right and that you will be with him until he feels better. In the beginning, it will actually be more important to talk calmly and softly–but consistently–until he again feels connected. When he begins to calm down, then it will be time to revert back to using your Sacred Listening skills. Let him describe what happened and allow him to work through his feelings. Try to help identify the triggers that first caused the panicked feelings so that those triggers can be sought out and dealt with before another emergency is allowed to happen.

The Seeker can be taught to take a kind of "time-out" when such triggers are encountered and frightening feelings start to arise.

After the actual emergency and after the Seeker has had time to calm down, both of you should decide on a time when you can have an advising session to discuss in more detail what happened and what spiritual truths could be learned from the experience. As frightening as they may be, spiritual emergencies usually arise from having to encounter a stark spiritual truth that the Seeker may or may not be prepared to face. That spiritual truth needs to be dealt with in any case since its appearance usually means that it is a lesson that needs to be learned. Often that truth will be veiled in symbolism and allegory but the symbols and stories are always related to the person who sees them. It may take some time and patience but a calm review of the experience and a discussion of the concepts behind it will eventually bear important spiritual fruit and the realization of those truths will help to dispel future spiritual emergencies. If the Seeker is not already part of a supportive spiritual community, then he should be encouraged to join one. It will help to be in the company of others who have had similar experiences or who can help people work through complex spiritual imagery.

Depression

Depression is a serious mental illness that can severely debilitate a person's life. Depression can come on in different degrees and stages. There is a difference between severe depression and mild depression. Almost everyone suffers from some sort of mild depression in their lifetimes–especially after something is lost. Mild depression can last anywhere from a few days to several months while serious depression can last for months or years. The main difference between the two is not the time spent in the state of depression itself. In a state of mild depression, a person can continue on with life even though she may not be as enthusiastic or active as before.

Depression is not considered severe until the person ceases to be able to do basic life tasks. A severely depressed person will miss a great deal of work or school or may not complete chores such as paying bills or cleaning up. Continued severe depression can eventually lead to a person to lose their home, their livelihood, and their close relationships. Both mildly and severely depressed persons will be fatigued due to a lack of sleep or will have unusual sleep patterns. They may have appetite or gastrointestinal difficulties due to poor or changed eating habits or to internal physical tension. These problems may lead to drastic changes in weight. Depressed people are also prone to drastic mood changes. They may have difficulty focusing or concentrating on anything.

Steps for Depression

- *Determine the degree of depression*
- *If severe, encourage the person to seek professional help*

Dealing with depression takes extra patience and strength and it takes a certain amount of wisdom and understanding to be able to get the person additional help, if needed. If a Seeker shows signs of depression but those signs do not indicate interference in the person's ability to continue with life, then you may consider trying to help. If, however, there is any indication that the Seeker is unable or unwilling to perform daily life functions then he needs to be referred to a helping professional.

In a spiritual sense, mild depression can sometimes be seen as a desire by the inner self to let something die. There may be an old habit, belief, value, or rule that was learned in the past but is now in the way of allowing further growth. In an advising session, the Spiritual Advisor can listen to a depressed Seeker and pay attention to discover what is it that needs to be let go. Letting go of a part of the self will require a change in the definition of the self. Not heeding the call can lead to a sense of meaningless that is the essence of depression. You can help lead the Seeker to that work and recognize that depression is only a need to eliminate a detrimental part of the self and not the whole self. Unfortunately, some people do not recognize this and believe that the symbolic call to death is a call for suicide.

Suicide

If a personal crisis or a state of depression seems so overwhelming to someone then that person may consider suicide. Suicide is a very serious issue and should never be taken lightly. If you suspect that a Seeker plans to harm himself or others then you should get help from other professionals. Sometimes an Advisor may find herself called upon to help someone who may be contemplating suicide. If that is the case, then she will need to help that person as best as she can until additional help can be sought. People who consider suicide as a way of escaping life's pressures can feel a deep sense of hopelessness. They can experience deep and lasting grief or anger, they may feel socially isolated in a painful way, or they may simply have a lack of enthusiasm for living.

When dealing with someone who mentions suicide in a conversation, it is important to take what the person says seriously and not immediately dismiss it. People sometimes talk about suicide as a way of calling for help without actually intending to commit suicide but the Advisor should never assume to know the true intent of the person. As in any crisis situation, the first order of business is to try and remove the person from the dangerous situation. In a possible suicide situation, the person may have chosen the dangerous situation for himself in which case you will need to convince him to remove himself from that situation. Having someone to talk to is all that person might really need and the person may be convinced to come away from that situation so that a conversation can begin. Most importantly, if you are contacted by a person considering suicide, remain in contact with that person as long as you can and try to get help to that person as soon as possible. Be as calm and comforting as you can be so that person can be reassured through your strength. When the immediate situation has been resolved, be sure that the person receives help afterwards and that care is ongoing.

Stages of Suicide

- *Withdrawal*
- *Contemplation*
- *Resolution*

In the early stage of suicide a person will become overwhelmed with intense feelings such as grief, loneliness, depression, and hopelessness. The crisis may be due to a particularly challenging situation or it may be due to emotional or physical reasons. Severe depression can be genetically or biologically influenced. A person may withdraw from routine life tasks and acquaintances as he tries to deal with the strong emotions and feelings. At this stage, a person is more likely to seek help and suicide will be considered as one of several possibilities for finding a sense of peace and resolution.

If the person is unable to resolve his dilemma he may then begin to seriously consider suicide. At this stage, he will begin to develop an actual plan involving a method and procedure that is possible to complete. He will still be wrestling with the anguish of his dilemma and may still be fearful of dying. If the person still cannot resolve feelings of hopelessness and cannot or will not seek help, he may enter the final stage of suicide where he will be resolved to go through with the actual act. A full and complete plan will have been developed and he will seek to go through with that plan. At this stage, the person believes that he has fully resolved all conflicts and will actually display a sense of calm and peace. Some caregivers have been fooled into believing that the person has changed his mind when in actuality he has simply made up his mind up to complete the task. The goal of the helper is to try and take intervention in the first or second stage of suicide when there is still some desire to continue with life.

Exercises

Solo Exercises

Solo Exercise no. 1 - Care for the Dying

Write out your experiences with someone you knew who was dying.

1. How did you handle the grief?
2. What would you do different?
3. How would you help someone else?

❈

Solo Exercise no. 2 - Crisis

Write out your own experiences with a spiritual crisis.

1. How did you handle it?
2. What would you do different?
3. How would you help someone else?

❈

Solo Exercise no. 3 - Depression

Write your own experience with depression.

1. How did you handle it?
2. How might you deal with it now?
3. How would you help someone else?

❈

Solo Exercise no. 4 - Suicide

Write your experience with contemplating suicide by yourself or someone you know.

1. What were the causes of the situation?
2. How did you handle it?
3. How would you help someone else?

Partner Exercises

Partner Exercise no. 1 - Care For the Dying

One person should discuss a real or imagined experience with being with a sick or dying person. The partner should practice Spiritual Advising techniques. When you are done, discuss your experience then switch roles.

❈

Partner Exercise no. 2 – Crisis

One person should discuss a real or imagined experience with a spiritual crisis. The partner should practice Spiritual Advising techniques. When you are done, discuss your experience then switch roles.

❈

Partner Exercise no. 3 - Depression

One person should discuss a real or imagined experience with a spiritual crisis. The partner should practice Spiritual Advising techniques. When you are done, discuss your experience then switch roles.

❈

Partner Exercise no. 4 – Suicide

One person should discuss a real or imagined experience with a someone who may have considered suicide. The partner should practice Spiritual Advising techniques. When you are done, discuss your experience then switch roles.

Chapter Two: Spiritual Growth

What Is Spiritual Growth?

T his section will discuss the process of spiritual growth. This is something that both Seeker and Advisor may benefit from knowing about and practicing.

Spiritual Growth is the practice of furthering a personal spiritual practice. In Spiritual Growth, someone seeks to find a way to add spirituality to all aspects of his daily life. In this way, living itself becomes a spiritual practice. Advisor and Seeker can both be students of spiritual growth

---

Purposes of Spiritual Growth

- *To clarify one's understanding of the sacred*
- *To deepen the relationship with the sacred*
- *To foster personal spiritual growth*
- *To integrate spiritual understanding with everyday life.*

Spiritual Growth must begin with some understanding of spirituality that reaches beyond the self and that connects us all. Once that understanding is clear, the Student can then learn how to deepen his relationship with his understanding of the divine.

Possible Results of Spiritual Growth

- *A connection to the sacred*
- *A meaningful and purposeful understanding of life*
- *A workable set of ethic*
- *A passion for life*
- *A desire to help others*

Besides developing a connection to the sacred, Spiritual Growth can deepen the personal spiritual growth of the Student. A connection between two power sources can only be as strong as those sources. Once the Student has determined his own understanding of the divine and begins to make a personal connection with it, he also has to develop himself as a spiritual person so that the energy between source and subject can flow freely. Once this connection between divinity and the spiritual person has been made, then Spiritual Growth can take place.

The last goal of Spiritual Growth is to help the Student learn to incorporate what she has learned and practiced in her daily life. Spiritual pursuits are empty if they cannot help us to make our lives and the lives of others more meaningful and enriched. These things can be developed through regular spiritual practices.

Seeking Spiritual Growth

People seek Spiritual Growth for many reasons but the connecting thread for those reasons is a desire to deepen a person's spirituality.

Reasons to Seek Spiritual Growth

- *To seek clarity in spiritual matters*
- *To deepen a relationship with the divine*
- *To further spiritual growth*
- *To integrate spiritual values into life*

Whatever the reason, Spiritual Growth can help people deepen their personal faith in profound ways. Spiritual Growth, in fact, can be seen as an important supplement to spiritual classes.

Everyone has spiritual needs and ignoring those needs only leads to future difficulties in life. These needs are what calls us to seek answers about things that are beyond ourselves–things that are much greater than separate individuals–that is to say, spiritual questions.

People have a need to have some philosophy of life that helps them to answer the big questions like "Who am I?" or "What is my purpose in life?" Besides spiritual communities, people also need to be in a relationship with other people like friends, coworkers, and family members. How we relate to each other depends a great deal on how we view the universe. People also need to feel some connection with whatever it is they believe to be the ultimate reality of the universe. Otherwise, a person can feel disconnected and insignificant. Feelings like these can lead to deep emotional challenges in life.

People crave to be in community with other people of like minds. This is especially true for religious communities. Even solitary people often find themselves wanting to at least talk to others who believe similar theologies. A spiritual community does not always have to be a church or other religious building in which to congregate. Spiritual community can take place in classes, impromptu get-togethers, cyberspace, or in any other way that people can come together to share ideas and support each other.

Spiritual Growth can help a person develop and strengthen all these spiritual needs.

Difference Between Spiritual Growth and Counseling

Spiritual Growth and Spiritual Advising have some similar goals but are different activities. Spiritual Advising seeks to help someone work through a specific problem or challenge. Spiritual Growth seeks to help someone examine their whole spiritual life. At the very least a Student of Spiritual Growth will have had some experience in developing and practicing their beliefs and values and may be in a stable enough position in his life in order to pursue Spiritual Growth.

As in many forms of development, Spiritual Growth happens in stages but not everyone goes through all the stages. A person can be physically mature and spiritually immature at the same time. The Student needs to understand these stages and the process for encouraging spiritual growth through them, not so that she can judge or categorize others, but so that she can move to the next stage of development. These stages of development will be discussed in detail in this section of the book.

The person who desires to undergo Spiritual Growth will have a different purpose than the person seeking Spiritual Advising. The person seeking advising will be in a state of short-term crisis and will need to find a resolution to that crisis through his spirituality. A person seeking Spiritual Growth will be interested in spiritual learning and will desire to learn how to apply that learning to daily life. There are no quick fixes or instant winners in the process of spiritual growth. The Student must be willing to endure the pangs of learning and growing and be willing to try new things regardless of how strange they may seem.

Spiritual Development

Introduction

When seeking Spiritual Growth it is necessary to have a general understanding of where one is is in his spiritual journey. In this chapter, we will discuss levels of spirituality and the process of spiritual growth. Talking about levels, however, can be problematic. Levels and stages carved out by philosophers and social scientists are arbitrary because they try to put people into neat little boxes. The difficulty with these delineations comes from the fact that all people are different. No one fits neatly into any one box. Every person develops at their own pace and in their own way–if they develop at all. However, there are clearly some similar traits and characteristics that people share in their progression to develop and grow and it helps to be able to recognize those traits in the people you are trying to help.

We are concerned here only with spiritual growth so we will look at how people learn to identify, connect, and interact with the world beyond themselves. By being able to recognize where a person is on the path to enlightenment we can know where the next step for them may be.

Stages of Spiritual Development

- *Egocentric*
  focused on self
- *Conventional*
  focused on group identity
-   *The family*
     Small groups of friends or loved ones
     Affinity groups
     Identity groups (race, gender, etc,)

> _Nationality_
> - _Mystical_
> _focused on unity_
> _The world and the self are one_
> _Nature and the self are one_
> _All things and the self are one_
> _All things are one_
> - _Undifferentiated_
> _Experienced as no difference between self and all things_

It should be carefully noted here that these levels are meant to help the Student discern where they are in their spiritual path. These levels are not meant and should never be used to judge one person from another. A person further along on a spiritual path is not better than one less developed. These stages are not to be used as personal value judgments; they are tools for helping progress and nothing more.

The theory of spiritual growth I am going to discuss in this chapter is mostly my own though it has been developed through the study of many philosophers and social scientists and through the observations I have made in my own work with people. It is only one theory and I suggest that you become familiar with as many as you can. The bibliography of this book lists several authors who have done work in this area including Fowler, Helminiak, Kegan, Underhill, and Wilbur.

The work of human spiritual growth is a complicated matter but I have worked to make this theory as straightforward and accessible as I can. The discussion will begin with the concept of three drives or forces of motivation that move us to do certain things in our lives. It is important to recognize these three strong drives and the desires they create within us in order to understand why we do the things we do and how we can balance those needs and desires.

One of those desires is a connection and relationship to the divine which can be accomplished through the process of spiritual growth and awareness. Enlightenment, however, is not something that happens overnight; it is a slow and gradual process of growth. Several researchers have assigned various levels or stages to the process of growth but development happens along a gradient, not in blocks or steps. Whether that developmental slope is cut into two slices or twenty does not change the actual process–only how we look at it. I have chosen to look at the process in three stages or levels which certainly leads to gross generalizations but I have found it better to begin to understand spiritual growth by looking at larger slices first and then allowing people to make their own subdivisions as they choose. We will look at some of those possible subdivisions as well.

Spiritual growth does not happen at a smooth and steady rate. I called it a gradation in the previous paragraph which might lend an image of a smoothly surfaced uphill road but the image of a dirty, bumpy, dusty, potholed, and twisted mountain trail might be more realistic. Growth can be both highly exhilarating and frustrating at the same time and moving from one level to the next can be a painful process because it requires a transformation of the self. All growth involves experiencing growth pains. Besides discussing three stages, I will also mention the four step process of transformation that often takes place when a person moves from one level to the next.

It is also important to remember that spiritual growth is a process of developing wholeness. Growth must happen with the whole self. Just knowing about spiritual concepts is not enough; feeling spiritual without being spiritual is not being wholly sacred. Wholeness involves developing all the different parts of the self. I will discuss the parts of the self and we will look at the role of these parts of the self in promoting wholeness in spiritual growth. Lastly, I will also discuss some of the qualities of what I believe to be the integrated self or the person who has made great progress in spiritual growth so that you may envision a model of growth to use in encouraging others to develop.

The Three Drives

Earlier in this work I mentioned three forces that are constantly at work within us: Agency, Communion, and Security.

Agency is the drive that calls us to be unique individuals. Through it we create and express our views; we determine our careers, life choices, and spiritual paths; and we desire to experience life and be our own person. It is the drive that can make us want to be whole, healthy, and happy.

Communion is the drive that calls us to be with others. Through it we seek partners in life and join with others of similar interests and pursuits; we create families, clubs, societies, and nations; and we desire the joy and protection of sharing with others. It is also the drive that can cause us to seek connections and interconnections and to seek our original source. It is what creates our hunger to seek the spiritual.

Security is the force that causes us to settle, to seek routine, and to rest and renew. It is also the force that resists change and is the reason that change must happen slowly so that changes can become integrated. The greater the change, the more time is required to adapt to that change. The need for stasis in our lives creates in us the desire to maintain balance and seek familiarity. In the pursuit of spiritual growth, the drive of security calls us to integrate new realities into our life and demands that our practice be practical and enriching.

It is important to remember that each of these drives is

important. One may be emphasized over another for a time but, like trying to stretch a balloon, one part can only be pulled so far before the rest will be strained. Some practices focus solely on selfless relationships while ignoring the need to maintain a healthy sense of self. A spiritual growth that emphasizes a balance of forces can help us to expand the concept of the self until it embraces all of life and all existence.

Only after this process of gradual expansion is complete can we then begin to glimpse a view of the divine. This is done by redefining the concept of self until we experience the unity of all things. This experience of the sacred, though, often happens in a fleeting moment. Though it may seem like an eternity at the time of its occurrence, rarely does the actual time spent in this type of ecstatic state last. These spiritual events are called peak experiences and they are brief because Agency always calls us to return to individuality so that we may continue on with life. Those who do not return from the peak experience spend all their time being in love with the divine and disregard their own need to survive. There is literally no one home to do the work of caring for self and others. Such an ascetic dedication to the divine may be fine for a few but would not be healthy for the larger community.

Security resists the change required to enact the process of spiritual growth but do not make the mistake of viewing that as a purely unfortunate thing. The resistance that security creates is necessary to keep us from just wandering about aimlessly without finding any real direction or meaning. Someone may be encouraged to mine one or more spiritual paths for truth and meaning and to incorporate those things into a spiritual life but, at some point, the weary traveler must find a home. Security resists the call to seek the sacred in fear that it may destroy a carefully constructed self-image.

Regardless of what theory one may study, what sacred text one may read, or what teacher one may follow, all agree on one point: the key to spiritual growth is to move beyond the personal ego into identifying with the greater divine. Spiritual growth is about the expansion of the self. Through Agency we seek to express and develop the self but the image of who we are or who we can be may be altered. We can change from being completely self-absorbed into becoming compassionate and spiritually aware beings. This is the process of spiritual growth.

The Three Levels

The three levels are an arbitrary way of dividing up the process of spiritual growth from being a self-centered person to becoming a universally connected being. These levels, however, can help us to recognize certain traits of spiritual growth and identify that may be needed to encourage growth. I will use the following words for these three levels: Egocentric, Conventional, and Mystical. Each is based on an expansion and then a contraction of the Self.

At the **Egocentric** level, the person is focused primarily on himself. At the very base of this level, the Student is concerned only with his own needs and desires. All interactions are designed to help him satisfy his own necessities and cravings. He reacts only to the things that reward him and avoids those which cause him pain. He is completely dependent on others to set limitations. Any small amount of care he may have for others (which can increase slowly) will come in the form of sympathy–feeling sorrow for those who go through pains he has already experienced. His spirituality will be purely personal and he will engage in whatever practice he believes will help him gain what he desires. His image of the divine will be one that is but a mere extension of his own self or his world. It may be a father-figure God or loving-mother Goddess or an angry alter ego of his own personality.

At the **Conventional** level, the Student expands the feeling of the connection of the self in an outward direction. She begins to identify with small groups like the family. The expansion continues as she develops social skills and learns to connect with groups of friends, her school, her neighborhood, and so on. Shee begins to identify with and adapt for herself group values.

Her sense of right and wrong is legalistic. In other words, she acts in certain ways because that is how other people do it. Authority figures are group leaders or others so identified by society. She begins to develop empathy or the ability to be concerned about the pain of others regardless of whether or not she has experienced similar pain. She develops a desire to want to help others though she is mostly concerned with helping people around him such as family and friends.

Her spirituality becomes dependent upon learning the religion of her family and culture. Her concept of the divine is based on what she has been told or learned it should be though she may or may not fully comprehend the concepts. She will identify with a particular sect of a religion and claim that only they know the real truth. At this stage of development, she will adopt a set of standard ethics and a spiritual practice based on her chosen religious group. For her, all symbols will be literally understood as having a singular correct meaning. It should be noted that this is the stage where most of the world (about 70%) can be found.

Those who push to develop past the Conventional stage enter into the third stage: the **Mystical.** There are at least two main reasons that most of the world is at the Conventional level. One is that it is a comfortable place to be. When you identify with a group of people, that group reinforces itself and provides support and comfort for its members. People at this level can also still maintain some independence (depending on their group associations and requirements). Therefore, people can satisfy both their needs for individuality and group identity. The second reason is that further spiritual development requires a different approach. At the higher end of the Conventional level, the person can begin to identify with larger concepts such as the world or even the universe but development cannot go any further until that person begins to learn to let go of the ego. The self must now not expand but diminish.

At the Mystical stage, a person begins to identify more with the world and diminishes his identity with the personal ego. He begins to see wrong and right in terms of universal concepts and principles that go beyond human laws and customs. His sense of authority comes not from other people but from deeply held beliefs that have been considered and analyzed over a long period of time. Likewise, his spirituality is defined by his personal beliefs. Even if he follows a standardized religion, it is because he has carefully thought about the tenets of that religion and have embraced them as his own. He does not simply and blindly accept the truth of others.

Religious symbols are, to him, figurative. He understands that they are representative and complex and he can determine his own meaning to their significance. He develops compassion or the ability to care for all beings regardless of their challenges in life. He feels a deep need to help others in the world and feels no need to get credit for his work. He is able to find joy in small things, to forgive, and to finds ways to incorporate his understanding of the universe into his daily life activities. A curious paradox is encountered at this level, however. Though the ego self–the self that is concerned with personal desires and daily worries–is diminished, another side of self continues to expand. There develops a kind of split between the ego self and what many term the "higher" self. This higher self is more concerned with universal compassion and divinity and can eventually merge with the person's self identity.

There is yet one other level. I call this other level the **Undifferentiated.** It comes both before and after the three levels discussed above. We come into this world as infants at the level of the Undifferentiated. At this stage, there is no difference between the self and the world; there is no concept of an individual self. As infants, we are totally dependent on our parents and caregivers to provide all our needs. Interaction with the world is done simply through reflex and instinct. The Undifferentiated infant is either not capable or does not yet realize that she has the ability to make choices and that those choices can affect the world around her. That moment of realization has been dubbed "the existential moment" and is the first defining personal crisis that brings a person into the stage of the egocentric.

The curious thing about the Undifferentiated level is that this sense of non-identification with the self can also be experienced at the highest end of the Mystical stage. In fact, it is often the goal of the spiritual seeker at that level. A person at the Mystical stage can experience brief moments or even extended periods of self dissolution when only the unity of all things or an experience of the divine is felt. There is no longer a separation between the knower and the known, the subject and the object, or the experience and the one who seeks the experience. For a rare and short time, there is only the stark reality and existence of now. It is at these moments that the purity and innocence of the child becomes the wisdom and enlightenment of the spiritual seeker. The journey ends where it begins but the person who has had this experience may feel reborn and live differently. Spiritual realization is incorporated into daily life and the fear of death disappears. The cycle of spiritual development becomes complete.

	SPIRITUAL LEVELS	

	Egocentric	Conventional	Mystical
Identification	the Self	with others	the world
Moral Judgment	Punishment/ reward	social/ legalistic	universal law
Authority	dependence	groups	principle
Symbols	personal	literal	multi-dimensional
Concern	sympathetic	empathetic	compassion
Responsibility	helping self	helping others	helping the world
Divinity	extension of self	extension of others	all is one
Spirituality	personal	sect-oriented	universal
Values	love of self	love of others, ethics, belief system and practice	love of all, forgiveness, integrated practice

At each level of spiritual development, the three drives are present. The drive of Agency gives the undifferentiated child with the will to survive and pursue her needs to continue growth.

At some point, Agency breaks through the fog of pure reactivity and we come to realize we are independent thinking beings with choices to make. Life can go on quite fine at this Egocentric Level if you pay no attention to the people that you anger in the process of ignoring their needs and desires.

Eventually, though, Communion can intervene and make us

realize there are others out there who have needs and desires similar to our own. We realize that survival depends on the help of others. We learn to cooperate out of necessity but, eventually, we can learn to genuinely care for those others. A need to be a part of groups helps us to expand our care to larger and larger circles while it also allows us the room to begin to expand the concept of ourselves.

Communion can only get us so far on the spiritual journey, however, as one reaches the end of the Conventional Level and begins to move into the Mystical. It is the call to a greater love, a love that can engulf the whole universe, that starts one on the path to the Mystical level of realization. A fully developed self with confidence and strength is allowed to diminish itself slowly until the totality of the divine is experienced with whatever spiritual map or system the Seeker may need. Though we are meant to seek the Sacred we are also meant to live and survive. The desire for the ultimate love must be balanced with the need to continue to live and experience the multi-faceted adventure that is life.

As I mentioned earlier in this chapter, it is possible to think in terms of more than three levels. Many of the authors of books on this subject have identified from three to ten levels. I have outlined three to make it simple but have also chosen to mention sub-levels of each stage. In the Conventional level, the expansion of the self happens in ever widening circles, each of which can be considered a smaller level of spiritual growth. Movement from the Egocentric to the Conventional often happens by recognizing the self in the form of love and care for another person. As we desire care and nurturing so we recognize that others need those things as well. Eventually, the circle of loved ones widens and identification with others expands as well. The Conventional level could be subdivided by these types of groups.

The Mystical level can also be subdivided as the higher self expands beyond human groups and toward the mysteries of nature and the universe.

I will be the first to mention that there are several problems with this theory as there are with all theories but mentioning them here will help you to form your own solutions and it will, hopefully, keep me humble. First of all, using only three levels to identify the long and complex process of spiritual development is too vague and general but I use it to keep things simple. Observing sub-levels can help add some complexity to the system, however, and reading other theories will help you to expand your own experience.

Secondly, people often see levels like stops on a rising elevator and this is just not the case; levels are simply more amorphous than that. All growth happens by learning and adapting new information and new experiences to an existing model of understanding. There must be both transcendence of the current life patterns and integration of the new patterns with the old.

Another problem with any such system of levels is that people grow at different rates and do not grow evenly. In other words, a person may intellectually know about the unity of nature and people but may be emotionally unable to feel that unity in his heart or be able to connect with nature within his soul. Just knowing about sacred concepts is not enough to be spiritual because knowledge affects only one part of the whole self.

The Three Parts of Self

We often act in contradictory ways because there is more to each person than just the single ego. There are three parts to the self and each has a way that it acts and reacts with the environment. Depending on your spiritual view, you may want to add a fourth part which is often referred to as the soul.

Three Parts of the Self

- *Body*
- *Mind*
- *Heart*
- *(Soul)*

The **body** is the physical part of the self. It is what houses the rest of the self as it goes through life. It is primarily through the body and its senses that we experience most of the material elements of life.

The **mind** is our mental aspect. It is where our thoughts and memories are stored and expressed to ourselves and others. The mind has a physical counterpart called the brain but the brain does not constitute the entirety of mind. It is through the mind that we communicate and make meaning of the things we encounter.

Our emotional side is expressed through the part of ourselves we call the **heart**. Although we do have an organ called the heart it really has nothing to do with our emotions. The organ called the heart and the part of the self called the heart have little relation to each other. The emotional heart is where we learn to feel and react to situations. In an earlier part of our evolution, e-motions were external motions used to avoid dangers and find sexual mates. Now, of course, our emotions have become quite complex as our list of fears and attractions have increased.

At the Egocentric level, growth will be focused primarily on the body through self-image, and self-esteem. Movement to the Conventional level will be jump-started primarily from the heart as we learn to love more than just ourselves. There will be less concern about appearances but a strong and confident self-image will be important. As previously mentioned, growth at the Conventional level takes place through an expansion of the image of the self which is encouraged through caring for others.

Movement to the upper end of the Conventional level and into the Mystical level begins to happen through the mind as we learn about spiritual concepts. Asking questions and insisting on finding a personal truth is a way to progress to an individual understanding of and relationship to the divine. Being on the Mystical level, however, requires that we not just think about spiritual concepts. We must be able to feel them in our bodies and we must be able to feel a connection to things beyond ourselves.

Transformation

From reading the previous sections on levels of spiritual growth, you might get the impression that spiritual development happens on a smooth and consistent climb from self-awareness to universal consciousness. This is not so. Moving from one level to another or even from one sub-level to another does not happen smoothly. Since all these levels require new ways of understanding, feeling, experiencing, and interacting with the world, transformations from one to the other require major changes in self-image, philosophy, and consciousness. Going through those changes can be disruptive and frightening–depending on the level of preparation made beforehand.

Stages of Transformation

- *Awakening*
- *Purification*

- *Illumination*
- *Integration*

Several researchers have studied the process of transformation and have identified stages of change. I have chosen to base my stages of transformation on four of the five stages identified by Evelyn Underhill in her book on mysticism. Actually, I will mention all five of her stages but in a different order.

The first step called **Awakening** often begins with a crisis of some type that forces us to make a change in our consciousness. It is easy to feel comfortable in our current spiritual state and it can take a jolt in our lives to force us to make a change and grow. There are many things that can force this type of change upon us. Some of them we can control and some of them we cannot. Events such as the onset of disease, a medical operation, an accident, a physical crisis or catastrophe, or childbirth can present us with a sudden challenge to our understanding of the world which we may or may not be prepared to handle.

We can also encourage that change through spiritual practices such as through the many different forms of meditation. Anything that causes any one of the parts of the self to break through everyday habits into new and challenging experiences can lead to a call toward spiritual growth. After such an experience and the ensuing crisis it causes there may come an awakening–a realization that something must change for the better.

In the second step of transformation, **Purification,** the person undergoing spiritual change must clear out the old habits and thought patterns of before. Old ideas and ways of doing things that do not fit with the new idea brought about from the Awakening have to be pruned away just like the old branches of a tree. This can be a painful and disorienting step because it asks the person to begin to redefine himself. It is not unlike the snake that must occasionally shed its skin in order to renew itself. The old skin may have served the serpent well for some time but it must eventually be shed away so that a new more pliable skin can be brought to the surface.

The third step of transformation is **Illumination.** In this step, new patterns of thought are formed. There comes a clarity of vision and a strength in purpose. This is a joyous part of the transformation as fresh insight leads to a spiritual renewal. Like the newly emerged butterfly, the world of the illuminated becomes a new place in which to explore and play. A person at this stage becomes empowered by new knowledge and experience and looks for confirmation of the new viewpoint everywhere they look.

The final step of transformation, **Integration,** is often overlooked but is very important and it is this oversight that can lead to failure in the process of growth. After learning a new spiritual insight, it is necessary that the new vision be incorporated into the person's daily life. In essence, the guru must come down from the mountain and enter into the village. There is a Zen proverb that says, "Before enlightenment: chop wood, carry water. After enlightenment: chop wood, carry water." What this means is that spiritual enlightenment does not change the fact that we still have lives to lead, responsibilities to meet, and challenges to overcome. It is just that these things will now be done with a new attitude and view of life.

Before enlightenment we are disconnected and unhappy. Afterwards, we learn to live with a new sense of joy and purpose. I would add to the Zen teaching, "Before enlightenment: chop wood, carry water. After enlightenment: chop wood, carry water, smile." The new way of looking at life that has been revealed through Awakening, Purification, and Illumination must now be integrated into life and must be done by incorporating the new paradigm with all four parts of the self. If this new reality cannot be merged with the old way of living then it becomes a passing fancy–a brief moment of rejuvenation that does not actually renew. The unintegrated person will shortly return to the same viewpoints and habits of before and will feel that the journey toward spiritual growth has been a failure.

These steps to transformation are what move us from one level of development to another. The process of transformation can begin with a crisis to any one of the four parts of the self but, eventually, the whole self must be involved with the transformation in order for it to be successful. The fact that transformation often begins with a crisis is very significant. It means that crisis can have a positive effect on overall growth. Every life challenge can become an opportunity for spiritual growth. If navigated successfully, the four steps of transformation will help the Student reach a new sub-level or level of spiritual awareness.

Of course, if spiritual growth were as easy as walking up three flights of stairs in a building then the world would be filled with mystics but the reality is not so simplistic. Spiritual growth is more like trying to make your way up three flights of crowded uneven stairs in the dark while the building is in the midst of a major earthquake. People often get stuck in a particular level because staying in one place is comfortable and because the inevitable obstacles are often very challenging to overcome. Each level of growth can have its own unique challenges and there are additional obstacles created when we do not allow all of the three drives to develop.

At the Egocentric level, personal growth is not possible if the natural human needs of survival are not met. No person can possibly focus on expanding the self if they are sick or hungry. The basic needs for food, shelter, clothing, and safety are necessary for normal living and are a prerequisite for the pursuit of inner growth. On the other hand, if a person cannot learn to separate the things in life that are needed from those things that are not needed, then the constant and endless pursuit of desires can also interfere with the ability to pursue spiritual development. Fear is also a factor in growth. Personal fears about expanding the self can limit the desire for personal exploration.

At the Conventional Level, the obstacles to growth come mainly from others. People at this stage begin to identify with their associations with other people. Group ideals can become a major influence in growth. If a person is concerned that he may be considered strange for pursuing spiritual truths (especially if they are different from the group's) that person may be unwilling to continue learning and may, instead, seek group approval. Some groups or social conventions can put pressure on people not to grow. Some of those who have not attained higher levels of spiritual growth would prefer that others not pursue those goals either so that a "status quo" of mediocrity can be maintained. Another condition that can impede growth that is brought on by others is the threat or reality of violence brought on by difficult living situations, oppressive authority figures, violence, or war.

At the Mystical Level people begin to look beyond themselves and their group associations. This leads to investigating the great mystery that lies beyond but seeking the unknown can be a fearful activity. At some point, we come to realize that the universe is a vast place full of mysterious wonders and that we are but a tiny speck in this great cosmos. We can become fearful of this fact or we can check our fears and learn to stand in awe of it.

The three drives mentioned earlier: Agency, Communion, and

Security must also be kept in mind during any stage of spiritual development otherwise the energy to grow will not be complete and the Student will become stuck. Security requires us to seek balance and stasis. All growth must be made slowly so that the system can adjust to the new changes.

Agency requires us to seek rest and confidence as we progress. If this is not done then the Student may experience exhaustion of the body, mind, or heart. If not properly dealt with, this exhaustion can lead to depression or failure or a desire to stop trying. Ignoring the need for personal expression and confidence can lead to self-doubt. The Student has to believe that he is making some kind of progress, however small, and needs to trust that he has the ability to succeed. The Student also needs the support and encouragement from others to help fulfill the drive of Communion or the need to be part of something larger than himself.

Spiritual growth is easier and more beneficial when it is done through the help and compassion of others. Learning to love and be loved is one of the many lessons learned along the way. The Student comes to learn that she is not alone and that the universe is filled with the love of other people. Without a system of support like a teacher or support group, the Student can feel isolated or become lost and search around aimlessly for long periods of time. Of course, some people find their way just fine by themselves but it usually takes a great deal more time and effort and requires a great amount of inner strength and personal confidence to go it alone. Not all are so lucky to possess these traits. A spiritual emergency can take place if the Student comes to experience too much without some guidance as to how to navigate the new territory.

Transformation must take place through all the parts of the Self but certain parts can be used to encourage growth. The body can be encouraged to seek union through states of physical ecstasy such as those that can be reached through dance, exercise, or certain physical movements. Being active with other people encourages growth beyond the ego self as connections and a sense of belonging are made with others.

The mind can be encouraged to seek spiritual growth through learning sacred and religious teachings, finding and pursuing a deep sense of wonder about the world and others, and through the contemplation of metaphysical issues and mysteries. The heart, too, can grow spiritually through loving and by developing and promoting compassion for the self and all others and through peak experiences. Spiritual direction is one way to help people seek those methods of spiritual development.

By honoring the three drives, and encouraging growth in the three parts of the self through the three levels and the four steps of transformation, the Student can become an authentic and balanced person. It can be helpful to have a model of what a balanced person may look like. We will observe the characteristics of such a person through the three parts of the self. These characteristics are ideals, of course, and few, if any people, will display all these characteristics all the time.

Through the body, the spiritually mature person has a strong and loving self image that is based in reality and not fantasy. Such a person knows her limitations and her strengths and is able to work with those abilities and challenges. She is not driven by unnecessary desires but is able to fulfill her basic needs and can balance those needs and desires. She is able to handle stressful situations and difficult challenges but is willing to seek help when needed. She works to take care of her body without being obsessed about it. She is responsible in accepting tasks and meeting her responsibilities. She enjoys being creative in whatever way is important to her and can successfully balance her activities with rest.

The spiritually mature person's mental characteristics include a generally positive opinion of herself, others, and the world. He accepts criticism and tends not to get angry or upset easily. His generally joyous view of life gives him little reason to be arrogant or jealous or to harbor hatred against others. He enjoys learning and enriching his mind. His philosophy for living and of life in general is lead by his positive spiritual values and are used to enjoy a full and rich life. He has worked to create a workable set of ethics that are both personal and universally acceptable.

Through the heart, the spiritually mature person has compassion for herself as well as for all beings. This compassion is revealed through a sense of patience and understanding with herself and with others. She enjoys working and being with others and can share in the joy and success of others. She has little reason to find blame and is generally able to forgive those who may hurt her. She is able to clearly express her needs and feelings to herself and to other people.

Exercises

Solo Exercises

Solo Exercise no. 1 - The Three Drives

1. Describe in writing a time when the drive of Agency influenced your life.

2. Describe in writing a time when the drive of Communion influenced your life.

3. Describe in writing a time when the drive of Security influenced your life.

❖

Solo Exercise no. 2 - The Three Levels

1. Describe in writing a time in your life when your spirituality was mostly egocentric.

2. Describe in writing a time when your spirituality expanded beyond yourself.

3. Describe in writing an experience that you might consider mystical in nature.

❖

Solo Exercise no. 3 - Transformation

1. Describe in writing an awakening experience that brought you on your spiritual journey.

2. Describe in writing a purifying experience in which you had to eliminate a sacred idea or habit.

3. Describe in writing an illuminating experience in which you embraced a new spiritual idea or concept.

4. Describe in writing an integrating experience in which you incorporated a new concept into your everyday life.

Partner Exercises

Partner Exercise no. 1 - The Three Drives

One person should discuss an experience with the drives of agency, communion, or security. The partner should practice Sacred Listening and Spiritual Advising techniques. When done, discuss your experience then switch roles.

❖

Partner Exercise no. 2 - The Three Levels

One person should discuss an experience with the levels of egocentric, conventional, or mystical spirituality. The partner should practice Sacred Listening and Spiritual Advising techniques. When done, discuss your experience then switch roles.

✳

Partner Exercise no. 3 – Transformation

One person should discuss an experience with the transformative process of awakening, purification, illumination, or integration. The partner should practice Sacred Listening and Spiritual Advising techniques. When done, discuss your experience then switch roles.

Spiritual Practices

One effective way to encourage spiritual development is through spiritual practices. Below is a list of some useful practices. There are many books available on these practices which can give a more detailed explanation but a brief introduction is offered so that the Student can have an idea of the intent of the practice suggested. The practices are listed in alphabetical order. As always, you should suit the practice as needed to help your Seeker.

Awareness Meditations

These meditations involve allowing the Student to slow down his body and thoughts and find the kind of inner silence and solitude typically found through meditation. There are four Awareness Meditations in which the Student is asked to become aware of only one part of himself. The Student should attempt to shut out the other parts as he becomes aware only of what his body, mind, or feelings are doing while he is sitting in the meditation.

Blessing All Things

The Student simply offers a personal blessing to everything encountered. An offering can be made by saying something like "I recognize that you, as all things, are sacred and I offer a blessing to you."

Confession to Self or Others

This can be done as a spiritual practice. Sometimes it helps to get something off your chest, especially if you feel that you may have done something wrong to another. Making an admission and a confession to yourself can help alleviate the guilt but a confession should never take the form of self-deprecation. To admit making a mistake is not the same as claiming to be worthless or inadequate. Making mistakes is part of being human and no one is less worthy than anyone else. Confessions need not actually be delivered to anyone to be effective. Sometimes a silent confession or a confession given to the universe can be just as effective.

Contemplation

Contemplation means to go into a state of deep thought. This act is actually a form of meditation as the Student shuts out all other thoughts except for those being considered for contemplation. There are many things that can become objects of contemplation. Symbolism and the meaning of art works, sacred stories or meaningful myths, sacred reading, difficult theological questions, and the nature of the divine itself can all become a focus for concentrated thinking.

Deity Devotions

This is a practice used by many religions. To devote to someone or something means to offer something without expecting anything in return. People may devote their lives to a cause, or a higher power, or to understanding something and do it because they are passionate about it. They can do these things without seeking to be rewarded for their actions. Doing devotions can help a Student escape from her own ego needs and desires and offer something to a higher understanding or a greater need.

Dream Work

Sleep can be a spiritual practice. Dreams are a powerful and personal source of symbols which can be mined for interpretation by taking careful note of those dreams.

Fasting

This can be a very challenging practice. The Student is asked to abstain from eating for at least 24 hours. For those who do not regularly go hungry, this practice helps us to appreciate the fact that we often take our next meal for granted and it helps us have compassion for those who cannot. Fasting can be dangerous, though, and should never be done without the consideration of one's health and supervision by a health practitioner.

Following the Breath

This is a form of meditation in which the Student sits and concentrates only on the movement of the breath within and beyond the body.

Giving Anonymously

With this practice, one experiences the true joy of giving without expecting any gratitude in return. The Student should be encouraged to give a needed item to someone they do not know and without any follow-up by the recipient.

Healing Work

This is usually done by people who have had special training in an area of healing but, with some practice, some simple healing skills can be taught to a Student to be used with another willing person.

Journaling

Journaling is an important practice recommended by many spiritual teachers. The Student is asked to simply keep a daily journal in which he records his thoughts. Journals are good for organizing ideas, reviewing practices, and observing changes over time.

A Journey Meditation or Pilgrimage

A pilgrimage is the practice of taking a trip to a sacred place. It is up to the Student to determine which place is sacred. The trip to the chosen location should be as much a part of the adventure as actually arriving at the destination.

Loving-Kindness Meditation

This is a Buddhist practice in which the Student meditates on developing compassion for all beings. It uses a changing mantra that focuses first on the self and then widens the circle of relationships. The Student can begin by speaking slowly words like: "May I be blessed. May I be healthy. May I be loved. May I be filled with joy." Since all people truly desire to be blessed, loved, and joyful, it is easy to experience these feelings. The practice then requires that these same feelings be extended to others by repeating the mantra but with simple changes. The Student can continue by saying: "May my family be blessed, etc. and continue with "May my friends be blessed..." May the people I know be blessed...." "May all people be blessed..." leading to "May all beings be blessed..."

Mantra Meditations

Mantras are meditations that ask the Student to repeat a short phrase over and over for a long period of time. The phrase given as part of the meditation (for example: "all emotions are my emotions)" should be repeated either aloud or silently while sitting comfortably. The Student should maintain the repetition of that phrase for as long as possible and concentrate only on the words and their meaning.

Martial Arts

Martial Arts have a long tradition of developing self-defense and control. They are also powerful spiritual practices. Some, such as Tai Chi or Chi Kung, can be used specifically as spiritual practices.

Mindfulness

This is another Buddhist practice that is simple to learn but very difficult to master. The Student is asked to do an activity but must concentrate solely on that activity while doing it. The great Buddhist master Thich Nhat Han uses the example of washing the dishes. As the Student is washing the dishes she is to focus solely on the sensations and activities of washing. Her thoughts are centered on only what she is doing. She may say things like: "I am washing the dishes," "I feel the warm water on my hands," or "I am rinsing the soap off the dishes," and so on. This practice can force the Student to remain in the present moment.

Om Chant

This practice asks the Student to repeat the sound of "Om" for as long as possible. He should feel the vibration of the body as the Om is being sounded. This practice is one of the most important for Hindus because they consider the Om sound as one of the first creations of the universe.

Prayer Beads

These are used by many religious traditions, including Christianity. The beads of a rosary, for example, are rolled between the fingers and the Student repeats a prayer as each bead is felt between the fingers. A similar practice can be done with other items such as a prayer rug, shawl, or wheel.

Prayer

Prayer is the practice of communicating beyond the self. There are many types of prayer. Students can ask for thanks, find forgiveness, ask for help to solve a problem, or seek a blessing.

Sacred Vow

A sacred vow is a promise made regarding how one will act in a spiritual way. Making a sacred vow helps to live a life dedicated to higher spiritual values.

Service to Others

Service helps us to focus on the needs of others rather than on personal needs. There is great joy to be found in helping another person out who may be in need.

Silence

This is another universally used spiritual practice. In our world of constant sound and talk, learning to be silent for one or more days can be an enlightening challenge. Silence forces us to go within and seek peace and to learn how to communicate without words.

Sleep Deprivation

This is another denial practice. Like fasting, the practice of sleep deprivation asks the Seeker to force herself to stay awake for at least 24 hours. There are changes in consciousness that happen when natural sleep patterns are not attained. The Student should take advantage of this fact and explore the state that is attained through this method. Sleep deprivation can also be a health risk, however, and should not be explored without the advice of a health practitioner.

Solitude

Solitude is a practice that asks the Student to set himself away from contact with all other people for one or more days. Doing so helps him to realize how dependent he may be on others. Being in solitude with none of the usual distractions like the television or the phone or the company of others forces us to come face to face with our own fears, worries, and inner thoughts. It is a detox of the mind and body which can be highly uncomfortable at first but well worth the effort.

Sacred Texts

The study of sacred texts and symbols can lead to new and interesting insights. Religious and spiritual symbols can also be studied.

Total Compassion

This is the ability to feel a completely selfless love for all beings. It is a difficult state to achieve and can be even more difficult to maintain but is an important step in learning to expand the self to include all beings.

Visualizations

There are three types of Visualizations that are used in this section. Each one asks the Student to sit and meditate silently while maintaining a particular vision in mind. The practice can be likened to watching a movie in the mind only the Student is in control of the actions of the film. In the Self-Expansion Visualization, the Student expands the image of herself first by an inch or so slowly continuing until there becomes no separation between the Student and the world. The Self-Dissolution Visualization does the opposite as the Student begins to shrink herself only a little bit at a time until she is encouraged to go down into the sub-atomic level and become infinitesimally small or disappear completely. The Emptiness Visualization asks the Student to try and maintain an image of complete emptiness in its purest state.

Walking Meditation

A Walking Meditation is done by slowly and deliberately walking while maintaining a centered and meditative frame of mind. Most often it is done in a peaceful place with few distractions. The head is pointed towards the feet or the ground and the hands are kept behind the back. Walkers can focus on the rhythm of their breathing or on the rhythm of the feet moving along the ground.

Letters

Writing letters of forgiveness or confession is a practice that can help relieve guilt or shame by making amends. Asking for forgiveness, forgiving others, and confessing mistakes can all be done without casting blame on yourself or others. Forgiving or confessing does not excuse an action. Instead, it lets the Student release caustic feelings toward himself. Writing down these things in a letter helps the Student clearly outline and articulate his feelings. Completed letters need not be sent to the recipient to be effective.

Working with Flowers, Plants, or Herbs

Gardening is a great way for the Student to work and connect directly with the earth. Helping grow things can make the Student part of the process of creation and there is no substitute for getting your hands dirty and touching the soil and the rich textures of plants.

Yoga

This is an ancient Hindu practice that involves the whole self in trying to be at one with Spirit. It is a practice that involves more than just getting into difficult body positions. It also includes meditative practices and ways to maintain health.

Exercises

Solo Exercises

Solo Exercise no. 1 - Spiritual Practice

1. Review the list of spiritual practices.

2.
Consider doing any with which you are unfamiliar or which would be helpful to you.

Partner Exercise

Partner Exercise no. 1 - Spiritual Growth Process

1. With a partner, practice advising for the Spiritual Growth process.

2. When done, switch roles.

Chapter Three: Sacred Circles

Introduction

A Sacred Circle is any kind of regular activity or gathering focused on a spiritual theme. Examples of these are meetings, classes, or other shared activities. Specific examples include study groups, theological classes, prayer groups, meditation groups, book discussions, hiking groups, affinity gatherings, etc. A specific type of Sacred Circle is sometimes called a small group ministry. The purpose of these is mostly to promote discussion through an environment of support and caring for the members of the group.

Examples of Sacred Circles
<ul><li>*Small-group ministries*</li><li>*Meditation Circles*</li><li>*Spiritual discussion groups*</li><li>*Sacred text study groups*</li><li>*Support Groups*</li><li>*Spiritual classes*</li></ul>

The focus of this chapter will be on developing and maintaining a Sacred Circle in its many forms. Though there may be different functions for each circle, many of them will share some common traits.

Starting a Sacred Circle

Starting a Sacred Circle is not really a difficult task. If you find that you start mentoring a student or people come to you for answers and ideas in their spiritual practice it may be easier for you to create a Circle where they can all gather at once and learn and share with each other or some people may express an interest in doing something together. In many spiritual communities, there are already procedures and formats in place to start learning groups and small group ministries.

Steps to Start a Sacred Circle

- *Define the purpose*
- *Define the particulars*
- *Define expectations*
- *Set up the initial meeting*
- *Promote*

Begin the process by first considering your purpose for the Circle. Why do you want to do this? What do you hope the Circle will accomplish? Be clear and honest with yourself about your purpose. Hopefully, you will want to teach or lead a Circle because you enjoy helping others learn and explore.

Questions of Purpose

- *Why do you want to do this?*
- *Are you ready to commit to such a group?*

- *Who do you hope will attend your Circle?*
- *What do you hope your group will accomplish?*
- *What do you hope to get from the experience?*

Once you have defined a purpose for the Circle, consider gathering together at least two like-minded people in an informal setting like a coffee shop or someone's home and talk about how a circle may be set up. In that first meeting, you should discuss your purpose with them and get their reaction to your plans. The discussion may help to refine and sharpen that purpose and allows others to share in it.

Planning Questions

- *Where will you meet?*
- *When will you meet?*
- *How often will you meet?*
- *Will the meetings be open or closed?*
- *What will be the length of the meetings?*
- *What will be the minimum and maximum number of people?*
- *How will you deal with difficult situations?*
- *How will you promote the Circle?*

Next, you should discuss the particulars of the meetings. Decide where, when, how often, and how long the meetings will take place. Try to make the meetings as consistent as possible. People can remember a Circle time that is regular and will become frustrated when the schedule is inconsistent. Decide who and how many people should attend. Will the Circle be open to anyone at any time or will it be closed to only certain people? Maybe anyone can join in the beginning but then the membership will have to be restricted. A consideration of the number of people is also important. More people at your Circles may feel good to your ego but may be detrimental to the goals of the group. A small group ministry or Sacred Circle should be limited to around ten people with five people being the minimum and fifteen the most that should be brought together. Any more or any less makes it difficult for the group to feel supportive and intimate.

It is also very important that you seriously consider and have a discussion about how problems with participants will be faced. Try not to make the mistake of waiting for something to happen then reacting. The results are rarely satisfactory. Instead, consider policies and procedures for dealing with difficult people.

After a general discussion about the format has taken place, then it is time to get down to specifics about the actual procedures of the Circle. A schedule of the group's activities should be drawn up. For example, if a Circle is to meet for an hour once a week and it has been determined that there will be time to create community, have discussions, do an activity, and then have a final summary, then specific times should be allotted for each part of the class. A possible schedule might include ten minutes for an opening activity and sharing, twenty minutes for discussion, twenty minutes for an activity, and the final ten minutes reserved for review and a closing activity.

Finish the meeting by coming up with the content for the first meeting and then make a plan to get the space for the Circle scheduled and reserved. You should also come up with a plan for promoting the activity. For many leaders, marketing is the least enjoyable part of teaching and running spiritual groups but it is necessary for attracting people to your circles. It can also be a very time consuming and expensive activity. Fortunately, in this age of the internet, there are more inexpensive methods of marketing than ever before but you should not throw out the old fashioned ways of marketing too.

The most effective form of advertising has been and always will be word-of-mouth. Talk up your plans to everyone and anyone you can think of who might be interested. Tell people in any spiritual groups to which you may belong. Talk about it on any social media or other online community pages. If you have an email list or a list of names and addresses of people who may be interested in your project, drop them a note. Hard-copy flyers are also still a good way to advertise. Well designed, bright, and informative flyers placed around the community can be effective in getting the word out. Consider putting posters up in community-oriented stores. There are also local papers, alternative papers, magazines, and other advertisement publications that list community events for free. Many areas have local access television channels that list events as well.

You could also do internal promotion by creating informational brochures and newsletters. If your Circles are fun and informative then your best salespeople will be those who come to your Circle and tell others about it. If they have information on hand to share, then all the better. Consider creating a brief guide about your group. Participants can pick these up when they come and distribute them to others. Consider also creating a newcomer's guide that tells new people about your circle and what to expect. Include contact information and encourage them to ask questions. Sometimes a new person can be assigned to someone who has been coming for a while to be an ambassador. The ambassador will introduce the new person to everyone, answer questions, and make sure that he or she feels comfortable with the group. Consider also publishing a regular newsletter that lets people know what is going on and what will be happening in the future. A newsletter helps people feel connected when they are away from the meetings. Another way to advertise and to promote unity within the group is to design and create materials such as hats, t-shirts, buttons, and other materials that mention the group.

Another necessary annoyance for many group leaders is the issue of money. Running group meetings can cost money. If your group is sponsored by a spiritual community then basic expenses may be covered through them but additional expenses may occur. In either case, it is important to consider what can be done to cover any expenses. There may be those things which you have to purchase for promotion. There may be money involved in renting a space and materials for the Circle will need to be purchased. There are costs involved with copying and printing. You should consider including some food and drink for the meetings. All these little things can add up.

If you do not wish to charge for your circles but are not supported by another organization then you should, at least, consider asking for donations. Doing so allows offerings from those who can afford it while others can attend the meetings for free if they cannot. Consider starting a checking account for the group so that you can keep track of what is collected and what is spent. Keeping good records helps you to avoid the charge that you are not being responsible with the donations.

Exercises

Solo Exercises

Solo Exercise no. 1 - Purpose

1. Answer the following questions in relation to a Sacred Circle you want to start.

   1. Why do you want to do this?

   2. Are you physically ready to commit to such a group?

   3. Are you mentally and emotionally ready?

   4. Who do you hope to have in your Circle?

5. What do you hope the group will accomplish?

6. Why do you wish to lead such a group?

7. What do you hope to get out of the experience?

2. Review your answers to these questions.

✳

Solo Exercise no. 2 - Meetings

1. Answer the following questions concerning your Sacred Circle.

   1. Where will you meet?

   2. When will you meet?

   3. How often will you meet?

   4. Will the meetings be open or closed?

   5. What will be the length of the meetings?

   6. What will be the minimum and the maximum number of people?

2. Review your answers to these questions.

✳

Solo Exercise no. 3 - Format

Answer the following questions concerning your Sacred Circle.

1. How will your purpose for the group best be served?

2. What will you do during the meetings?

3. How will the activities of the group reflect

your purpose?

4. How will the activities of the group relate to a spiritual tradition?

5. How will people be encouraged to participate?

6. What outcomes do you hope to achieve for the participants?

7. How will you determine if those outcomes have been met?

8. What materials and resources will you need?

❉

Solo Exercise no. 4 - Difficulties

Answer the following questions concerning your Sacred Circle.

1. What will be the expectations of each participant?

2. What will be the response to difficult situations when expectations are not met?

Partner Exercises

Partner Exercise no. 1 - Sales Pitch

1. Describe to a partner your idea for a Sacred Circle.

1. What is its purpose?

2. When and where will it meet?

3. What will be its format?

2. Describe to your partner why he or she should join it.

3. When done, switch roles.

❉

<u>Partner Exercise no. 2 - Challenges</u>

1. Describe and encourage a spiritual practice such as meditation to your partner.

2. Have the partner begin to act inappropriately.

3. Find a way to deal with the situation that is firm but respectful.

4. Afterward, the partner should comment and advise you on your reaction and handling of the situation.

5. When done, switch roles.

Sacred Circle Meetings

The Format

Now that your Sacred Circle has been planned, it is time to consider what and how you will actually run it. Begin with formulating a specific plan for your event.

<u>Parts of a Sacred Circle</u>

- *Preparation*
- *Opening*
  signal to start
  welcoming statement
  opening activity
  brief explanation of the group
  expectations
  sharing (the Check-In)
- *Main Section*
  presentation
  discussion
  questions

> *main activity*
> *new information*
> *ending*
> • *Closing*
> *review*
> *expression of appreciation*
> *homework*
> *closing activity*
> *fellowship (refreshments)*

Preparation

You should always plan to arrive early to your activity space so that you can make sure that you will be adequately prepared for the Circle. If you are using a space other than your own, then you will always need to make sure that the space is ready in time. Make sure that the space is adequately lit, heated or cooled, has enough chairs and any other equipment you may need, and is quiet and undisturbed. Prepare the space as you need it. Put a number of chairs into a circle and place all the teaching materials you need into the circle. Be sure to have your brochures and newcomer information sheets with you and to have a pen and paper to record notes and the names and addresses of new people. If you do any small opening activity, make sure you have brought along those materials as well.

Opening

When students first arrive to the space it is natural for them to begin sitting in the chairs and talking to each other and with you. People should be encouraged to come a little early for this reason so that you can begin and end your Circle on time. There should be some formal way to mark the end of casual conversation and the start of the class. This is done with a signal to start such as stating out loud that it is time to start or by making a sound such as ringing a bell. When the noise and excitement has settled down, the facilitator should offer a brief welcoming statement letting the members know that she is happy they are there and ready for an exciting meeting. Next should come an opening activity. This could be something simple like singing a song or chant that the group knows or by saying a prayer or blessing together.

It should be kept in mind that doing things like invocations and chants together can help build a sense of community and continuity but it can also alienate newcomers who will feel as if they are not part of the group. Every effort should be made to make new people feel comfortable either by sharing information with them before the meeting about the opening or by having materials available in class that they can look over beforehand. Some groups offer a brief newcomer introduction before the regular meeting to teach chants and invocations and to explain the particulars of the group.

Before the meeting actually gets underway but while the group is paying attention, the facilitator needs to offer a brief explanation of the goals and purpose of the Circle as well as the expectations of its members. This should be done at every meeting even if there are no new participants present. It never hurts to be reminded of why the group gathered together in the first place and of its central purpose before any activities begin. Furthermore, it is important that the expectations of how members will act and interact with each other be reinforced at each meeting. This set of important principles is sometimes called the Covenant of the Circle.

The next part of the class is sometimes called the Check-In as each person checks in with the group to talk about where they are in their life. Going around the Circle, each person introduces themselves by stating their name. If they are new to the group, they might begin by saying what brought them to the Circle. Each person should then speak briefly about what has happened in their lives since the group last met. This activity builds community as each person is introduced and people begin to learn about each other. It also encourages people to speak right away so that when the time for the discussion comes up, people will feel less insecure about talking. Since every person is expected to say something, people will not be as concerned about whether or not they should speak. The check-in also builds community by allowing people to talk about any difficulties they may be encountering in their lives (if they wish to share) or by allowing people to join in celebrating accomplishments. The group should be encouraged to celebrate or offer words of encouragement and help, if possible, to those who need it. Part of having a successful Circle is encouraging this sense of shared community.

Some groups also do a "spiritual" Check-In where they are asked to go around the circle a second time and talk about how their spiritual life has developed since the last meeting. They should address questions like: "How is your spiritual practice progressing?", or "How has your spirituality affected your life since the last class?" Again, the group should be encouraged to support those things that are brought up in the process.

After the Check-In, some brief announcements that concern the class can be offered and people in the group are also welcome to offer any announcements they wish to share. People often learn about events and activities that other members of the class are doing.

The last part of the opening sequence will be the announcements made by the facilitator. At this point you can briefly review the topic of the last class to remind people about what was done and to create some continuity to the current class. The topic or focus for the present meeting can be announced to get people to begin thinking about it. New people can be recognized and welcomed. They should be encouraged to sign up for information or added to the newsletter or information list. Finally, let everyone know what will be happening for the rest of the class to give everyone an overview.

Presentation: Questions

The next part of the class format for Circles will be the central section–the presentation of new material or activities. Even if the Circle is focused mainly on an activity rather than on learning, there is often some teaching element involved in most meetings. This section will be focused on teaching effectiveness.

The tendency for most teachers is to focus on using lecture (a narrative done by the teacher revealing new information to the students). Lecture is a useful part of teaching but it should be only one part of a complete presentation which should include questions for exploration, a chance for discussion, and an explanation of new information.

Begin the meeting with a set of open-ended questions that encourage reflection, exploration, and discussion. Open-ended questions are those that do not have a single correct answer. In fact, the person asking open-ended questions should not have an answer in mind. Avoid questions that start with: what is a/ the....? Instead, use questions that start with how or why. When seeking a definition, ask questions like: what is your definition of....? Notice you are not asking for a single answer but for an opinion. If a person is asked and then gives his or her own definition then that answer cannot be wrong though it can differ from other definitions. Another good question is to ask people to describe their experiences with something.

Questions to Open a Discussion

- *When I say (term or topic to be discussed), what do you think it*

> *means?*
> - *Have any of you ever had any experience with (topic)?*
> - *What did these experiences teach you or how did they affect you?*
> - *What is your understanding of (topic)?"*

After asking each question, allow some time for people to think about their answer before calling on anyone. Do not be afraid to add moments of silence to the discussion. Silence gives people time to think and encourages people to participate. Questions can be asked to the whole group for anyone to answer or you might go around the circle and ask each person to give an answer. Be supportive of every answer.

Presentation: Discussion

Hopefully, the questions you ask and the answers that people provide will lead easily to an open and exciting discussion. At that point, your role in the meeting becomes one of a facilitator.

> Tips for a Successful Discussion
>
> - *Stay focused on the topic*
> - *Give everyone a chance to speak*
> - *Make everyone feel comfortable*

It will be your job to see that the discussion stays focused, that everyone is given a chance to speak and share, and that people feel comfortable being a part of the discussion (even if they are only listening). You should avoid offering your own opinions during the conversation unless you are specifically asked a question. Allow the group to express and explore. Just as with Spiritual Advising and Sacred Listening, your role during this part of the meeting is to guide people towards seeking their own insights. Encouraging people to have an open discussion like this offers several opportunities for the participants.

A free discussion allows people to explore a variety of perspectives. If the conversation is done with respect and tolerance toward each person in the group, an increased sense of openness and awareness becomes possible. As the leader of the group, you should demonstrate through your own actions how to listen and act respectfully toward each person and his or her opinion. Students will view you as a model for how to act in the group. Apply the principles of Sacred Listening in the Circle.

There are some disadvantages to a discussion, however. The three main problems that can arise during an open sharing of ideas are personality, pace, and focus. Dominant people and shy people can challenge the natural flow of a good group conversation.

Possible Problems
• *Personality*
overly dominant people *overly shy people*
• *Pace*
too slow *too fast*
• *Focus*
drifting from the topic

A dominant person can try to control a discussion by speaking for a long period of time and make it difficult for others to offer ideas or rebuttals. This overpowering person (who can sometimes be the facilitator) wants to be the center of attention. He may seek approval or affection from the group or he may just be an energetic extroverted type of person who does not know when to yield. Some speak long and loud in order to convert others to their way of thinking–fearing the possibility of having to question their own beliefs. Most often they are just seeking approval in an inappropriate way.

Try to understand the motivation of the person who seeks to dominate the discussion so that you can deal with the problem by appreciating his needs. The problem of a dominant speaker can be dealt with by addressing the whole group and reminding them of the need to be respectful by limiting comments. Having a set of guidelines which are presented at the opening for the class is a good way to avoid some of these problems. When someone gets out of hand you can remind him of those guidelines. If addressing the group does not work, you may need to approach the person directly after the meeting and ask that he be mindful of others for the next class. If neither of these approaches works and the dominant person continues to aggressively dominate a conversation, you may have to resort to asking that person to leave the class or the group altogether. It is best to resort to that step only after all other attempts at reconciliation have failed.

Though shy people do not create the same disruptive effect as the dominant person, they can be equally frustrating when trying to have a good discussion. Often new people are shy but will open up in subsequent meetings once they become comfortable with the group and begin to feel accepted. Of course, you should do what you can to see that you and the group extend to them those feelings of being welcomed and accepted. A truly shy person, however, is one who repeatedly comes and remains afraid to speak at all.

There are several possible reasons why a person may not feel comfortable speaking in a group situation. Such a person may be very introverted and tend to process everything internally rather than by speaking aloud. She may be afraid that she will look stupid or foolish in front of the other people. She may just feel unable to answer the questions or to offer anything unique to the conversation (possibly because of feelings of inadequacy). She may have had bad experiences in the past with similar groups or discussion situations or she may feel that she will gain nothing from making a contribution.

Sometimes it is best to allow the shy person to just remain silent but, more often than not, many shy people do want to join in the discussion but need some extra encouragement and assurance from the facilitator and the group. You can encourage shy people and all the people in your group to talk by going around the circle so that everyone speaks, rewarding those who do speak by thanking them or complimenting them on their ideas and contribution. You can also encourage people to speak by finding something unique about each person and asking him or her to offer their own perspective and by avoiding punishing people for offering incorrect or different answers. It is important that everyone in the group feel that their contribution is respected and is worthwhile to the conversation.

It is precisely because these and other challenges can appear suddenly during the course of an interesting and engaging meeting that a contingency for such possibilities needs to be considered early on in the planning process. Of course, not every challenge can be anticipated. The way to avoid most problems that may arise are to remember to keep everyone active, comfortable, and engaged in the meeting and to demand respect and consideration for and from each participant including the facilitator.

A steady pace is another way to encourage a good discussion. The tempo of the talk should not feel either too fast or too slow. A person who dominates a conversation by not allowing others to speak or if no one feels comfortable speaking, then the pace of conversation will be slowed. Conversely, if people are not given enough time to talk about their ideas or to allow everyone who wants to talk to do so, then the pace will feel too hurried. The conversation should be like an old fashioned steam train. It should be kept on track and it should feel as if the talk chugs on at an even pace. The conversation may change speeds slightly as it goes up and down hills but the motion will be generally and evenly forward.

The same is true for the overall focus of the conversation. It is easy to get off track when several people are offering ideas. Some people like to move into tangential areas as their conversation drifts but it is important for you, the leader, to keep the group focused on the topic at hand. People will become quickly frustrated and disenchanted with the group if too many unrelated topics come into the conversation. Always keep in mind the purpose of the day's meeting.

Keeping on focus also requires maintaining a level of enthusiasm for the topic. As long as people are excited about exploring the topic through the questions and by learning new things, it will be easy to maintain a strong focus but if that enthusiasm is lost, people will quickly become bored and distracted. That consistent level of energy has to begin with the facilitator but quickly spreads throughout the entire group when they become engaged with the topic. Teaching free adult classes is different from teaching in a public school because adult participants are there specifically because they want to learn the material. Tap into that excitement and use it as the driving energy for the meeting.

Presentation: New Information

The next part of the presentation phase is to present new information to the group. This is often called the lecture although that word has come into disfavor lately. People often view a lecture as something long and boring that no one really wants to hear. We will simply call it a lesson.

Tips For Lessons

- *Be brief*
- *Be enthusiastic*
- *Create a clear outline*
- *Use visual aids*
- *Offer alternative perspectives*
- *Suggest ways to learn more*
- *Allow time for questions and comments*
- *Stay on track*

You want to present that lesson in an exciting and engaging way and, fortunately, there are ways to do that. One of the most important ways is to remember to keep the lesson short. This part of the meeting should actually be the shortest. In many circles, however, it is not. Facilitators can go on for hours talking about a subject they love and want to share with others, but my experience has been that people can listen intently for only about twenty minutes at most before they begin to drift off or look for some other kind of stimulation. I recommend that lessons not go on for more than 10 - 15 minutes at the most and, even then, that 10 minutes needs to be filled with things other than just talk.

The next most important part of giving a lesson is to be enthusiastic about the information your are imparting to your students. Enthusiasm is infectious but so is boredom. Participants are more likely to get excited about learning the information if they see that you are excited about it as well. When leading a regular weekly Circle, it is possible that you may not feel as thrilled about leading it every week. We are all human and we all have our ups and downs in life that affect what we do. When you come into a Sacred Circle meeting, though, you want to try and put those things away and be excited about your subject matter and about sharing it with your participants.

If you are feeling less than happy when you begin a meeting, you may want to do a short meditation or breathing exercise before you begin. You could think about why you wanted to start the Circle in the first place and recall your initial enthusiasm. You could also treat the meeting like a play or a show. Actors in a play or people who put on shows must put on the dramatic mask when they are in front of an audience. No matter what may be going on in their lives they must act the part. The show must go on! If you are really feeling lousy or do not feel able to lead a meeting, you should cancel it ahead of time instead of struggling to have the right attitude or energy level in the class.

During the presentation, you want to impart new information in a clear and concise way so that your members can easily grasp the concepts and learn the skills. To do that, your presentation should have an introduction, a main body, and a brief summary. Start the presentation by telling your participants what they are about to learn. I suggest that your lesson be written down first in clear outline form. Go over that outline in your introduction. Next, present the information in the order you have outlined. The outline helps you to maintain a logical order to your lesson. Back-up your information with handouts, worksheets, and other visual aids. Be clear about offering your own perspective (there is no such thing as a purely objective lesson) and then present some alternative perspectives as well. Discuss your sources and offer other ways that people can learn more on their own. Keep the pace moderate and always be willing to let them ask questions and make brief comments as long as the lesson stays on track. When the main body of the lesson is over, then briefly go over the outline again to remind people what was presented.

Main Activities

A Circle that is based on all talk can become boring very fast. All meetings should include some type of activity for the students that help to keep them interested and furthers their learning through participation. Activities do not have to be overly complex to be effective. Mostly, they should simply reinforce the topic of the meeting. Listed here are several categories of activities that can be used in Learning Circles with examples of each to help you apply them to your own meetings.

Art Work

The students create something such as a craft item or simple piece of art. Students can be asked to draw or paint or put something together with provided materials. The emphasis of this activity should be in expression without judgment.

Imitation

The students imitate the facilitator in a learned activity. This is a good activity when there are a lot of steps involved in learning.

Where Am I?

The students learn to find out where they are on a placement chart, map, graph, or other similar instrument of measurement.

Adaptation

The students learn a principle or technique and are asked to adapt it to their own style or personality.

Worksheets

The students are given a worksheet with questions on it based on the information presented. The worksheet asks them to think about certain parts of the lesson. After completing the worksheet, students can compare answers or discuss them together.

Puzzles

Students use concepts learned in the class to help them solve a puzzle such as a crossword, a word search, jigsaw puzzles, or other type of puzzle or challenge. There are several online resources to help turn a list of words into a puzzle.

Games

Students are given props and rules for playing a game together that reinforces a concept learned during the lesson.

Analysis and Interpretation

Students are given something to analyze on their own. After finishing their own analysis they are invited to share their ideas with the class.

Guided or Free Meditation

Students are asked to do a simple guided meditation that helps them personally connect to the concepts shared in the lesson. Instructions should be given on how to repeat the meditation personally for further exploration.

Prayer/Blessing

Students join together to relate to the divine and ask for blessings.

Role Play/Simulation

Students are asked to take on the roles of other people or are asked to act out a simulated experience.

Sorting

Students are given a set of cards or other items and a set of categories and are asked to place the cards in the correct categories as explained in the lesson.

Small Group Discussion

Break the group into smaller groups and assign each different subjects or questions for discussion. Have each report their results after a given time period.

Brainstorming

Give a question to the group then have them shout out answers which are put on a white board or other device. Observe the results after a given amount of time.

Bingo

Put answers to questions, or pictures, or concepts discussed into several 5x5 squares. Each square should have the words in different places. The center square is usually a free square but does not have to be. Hand out the squares to the participants then call out the words, or call out questions that use the words for answers, in a random order. Play like a regular Bingo game.

Closing

After the activity has been completed or the Circle time is nearly over, the facilitator should bring the meeting to an end in a way that encourages contemplation and reflection, invites continued learning, and brings closure to the group. The members should be seated together in the original circle. To bring the meeting to an end, the facilitator can do a quick review of what was learned and experienced–leading the participants into recalling the main points and events of the meeting. The facilitator might also mention the topic or focus for the next meeting so that members can think and plan ahead. Some small amount of time should be available for participants to ask any final general questions or make any comments.

The facilitator should also encourage members to continue to learn and practice the topic discussed and offer ways for them to do that. In effect, students can be given a type of homework that encourages experience to continue beyond the Circle meeting. The following are some examples of activities to do after the meeting.

Journaling

Students enter their experiences into an ongoing journal.

Collecting Notes

Students collect notes and any handouts from the meeting and begin sorting and collecting them together.

Field Trip

Students go to a location where they can learn more about the topic.

Engaged Practice

The students apply the skills learned in class in another setting.

Homework

Students do work beyond the lesson.

Research

Students learn more about a topic beyond the lesson.

When ready, the facilitator can lead the group in a final chant, song, or recitation of closing words. Any activity done at the beginning to start the session can be undone. For example, if a candle was lit at the start of the meeting it should be extinguished at the conclusion. A final parting blessing, prayer, or chant can also be offered to the students. Before the meeting is complete, the facilitator should also offer thanks to the participants for taking time out of their busy lives to come together and share with each other. One way for a facilitator to show their appreciation is to offer refreshments after the meeting. Not only does this give participants a chance to nourish themselves, it also allows for a continued interaction that is less formal and structured than the meeting. People can continue to ask questions and have conversations with each other.

Four Basic Principles

Leading a Sacred Circle is truly an art; it is not just a skill that you pick up one day. Every type of Circle is a challenge unto itself and facilitators are constantly learning how to prepare and lead them better. There are so many factors to being a good facilitator: you have to know your subject, you have to know the psychology of individuals as well as a group, you have to know how to deliver your activities and lessons in the most effective and stimulating ways, and so on. With all those things to learn there are a lot of different principles to keep in mind. For the Circle leader who may just be starting out, too much information is not helpful. I suggest beginning facilitators start out with four very basic principles for their Circles.

Four Basic Principles for Facilitating
<ul><li>*Keep them on time*</li><li>*Keep them on task*</li><li>*Keep them interested*</li><li>*Keep them busy*</li></ul>

It is important to start and end each meeting on time. Even if there is only one participant who shows up at the designated start time, resist the temptation to wait for all the others to show up. There more you do that, the more people will realize that they do not need to come on time because, after all, you are going to wait for them. This just creates a never ending cycle. The later you start, the less time you will have for your class and it is not fair to those people who did make the effort to come on time to have to wait.

The opening activities at the beginning of the meeting help to define a clear start for the class. People know when they are late because they will know that they have missed the opening activities. If you do the same type of opening and do it at the same starting time each meeting, people will recognize it as an important part of the Circle and will miss doing it if they come late.

It is equally important to end on time. You may feel that there is so much more to do, learn, and talk about at the end of the allotted meeting time but consistently going over time is inconsiderate to the participants. We live in a culture that values staying active and people lead very busy lives. Honor the fact that some people have carved out some time in their busy schedules to join your Circle by not going over the class time.

It is also important to keep the participants focused on the activity and the task at hand. Sacred Circles can develop into small social networks which is not a bad thing as long as the members can stay centered during the meeting time. Model the behavior you want from your participants. They will learn best not from lectures about how to act but by watching you. If your discussions drift off into personal diatribes that have nothing to do with the stated topic and you engage in activities that are distracting or even disruptive to the participants, then they will learn to do the same. Strive to maintain a balance between the contributions of all the participants and to also balance having a good time with completing the tasks you have assigned.

One of the difficult challenges in learning how to lead a group is to understand how to keep people interested and engaged. Even though your participants will, most likely, be there because they want to be, if you cannot keep their interest, they will begin to think about other things and lose their focus. You can keep their focus by being enthusiastic about your activity and by appealing to different styles of learning.

Learning Preferences

- *Listening*
- *Seeing*
- *Touching*
- *Moving*

Most people tend to favor one type of sensory input over others. Those types of input are called auditory (listening), visual (seeing), tactile (touching), and kinesthetic (moving). The sense that is emphasized most influences the way we experience the world. If you can structure your meetings so that all the senses are engaged, then you will have a Circle that can appeal to a variety of people and learning styles.

Auditory people focus on their hearing; they learn best by listening to voices or to music. They enjoy listening to lectures, hearing and making music, and talking. Visual people like to see things; they enjoy visual aids, handouts, posters, and watching things that move. Tactile people enjoy using their sense of touch; they like to handle things and will enjoy getting visual aids to hold, having objects to manipulate and play with, and doing arts and crafts projects. Kinesthetic people enjoy moving; they learn best when they are in motion and tend to get bored easily if they sit too long. They will enjoy any activity that has some movement involved no matter how little.

Every meeting should appeal to all types of people. This can be done by including different activities. For example, a meeting can have an opening and closing activity that asks people to stand and move, a time for questions and discussion, a brief lecture or presentation, a set of handouts or other visual aids, and a physical learning activity.

Exercises

Solo Exercise

<u>Solo Exercise no. 1 - Planning a Circle Meeting</u>

1. Plan a Circle Meeting that meets your purpose for a Sacred Circle.

2. Include any of the following elements in your planning that is appropriate:

    1. an opening activity

    2. a check-in

    3. a presentation of purpose and expectations

    4. a presentation of the topic or focus

    5. a discussion of the topic

    6. a presentation of new information

    7. a main activity

    8. a closing activity

Partner Exercise

<u>Partner Exercise no. 1 - Practice Meeting</u>

1. Practice having your Circle meeting with one or more people using the format you conceived.

2. Keep in mind the four principles:

    1. stay on time

    2. stay on task

3. keep them interested

4. keep them busy

Evaluation

You might put a great deal of time into starting up, preparing, and leading your Sacred Circle but how do you know if all that work was worth the time? How do you know if your effort was effective? If you want to continue to improve as a group leader and you want your Circles to be as good as you can make them, then you need to assess the effectiveness of the entire experience.

Types of Evaluations

- *Formal*
- *Informal*

You can use formal or informal evaluations as a means of assessment. Informal evaluations come from being observant and asking your own questions through casual conversation. One of the best times to do this is immediately after the meeting. Groups often find that after shared activities, people feel bonded and energized. They often want to stick around for some casual fellowship. For this reason, it is often a good idea to have some light food and drink available for people to enjoy together.

Even though the actual Circle may be over, the learning will continue into the time of fellowship. People will talk about the meeting and its subject matter and may feel like asking questions that they, for whatever reason, did not want to ask during the meeting. This is also a good time to do an informal evaluation. As people are talking and eating, mill about the room and see what they are talking about. Check their moods.

Do they seem happy and energized? Are they talking about the meeting? Are they asking more questions? Are they sharing their experiences with each other? Ask your own questions as well.

You can ask people what they thought about the experience. What did they like about it? What could have been done better? Pay attention to what is being said so that you can think about what you can do to improve your circle for next time. You can also do more formal evaluations that ask people to write down the answers to your questions. Formal written evaluations allow people to carefully think through their answers. Formal evaluations tend to be more thorough than informal questioning. In this chapter, we will look at how you can put together some formal evaluations to help you to learn to do a better job of leading your circles.

In order to be effective, evaluations should be done as soon after completing the experience as possible. You can ask people to remain afterward for a few moments to complete a questionnaire or you can have the questions available at the location where they obtain the food and drinks served after the meeting. Evaluations should be helpful to you as the facilitator so they need to be geared towards comments and questions that are instructive and constructive. The questions should not be too general and should help the reviewer be descriptive. If, after reading a set of evaluations, you find that you cannot determine any specific ways of improving a meeting, then the questions may need to be changed.

There are three specific things that should be considered when evaluating a class: the environment, the meeting, and the facilitator.

Three Areas of Evaluation

- *The Environment*
- *The Meeting*
- *The Facilitator*

Attributes Of A Good Environment

An effective activity space should have adequate furnishings (places to sit down that are comfortable but not so comfortable that people fall asleep), an adequate maintenance of room temperature so people are comfortable, and adequate lighting so people can see what you are doing. The Circle meeting space should be free of strong distractions such as bad odors, excessive noise, large windows that face out to busy scenes, and unrelated activities in the room. The room should also be well supplied and clean.

A Good Environment

- *Adequate furnishings*
- *Adequate temperature*
- *Adequate lighting*
- *Free of distractions*

Attributes Of A Good Circle Meeting

An effective Sacred Circle meeting should have at least four qualities: it should be enjoyable, informative, challenging, and enriching.

A Good Meeting

- *Enjoyable*
- *Informative*
- *Challenging*

- *Enriching*

An enjoyable meeting is fun for both the individual and the group. Meetings that include events such as questions, stimulating debate, a short lesson, and an activity will be more interesting than one that is just all lecture or is totally unstructured. Part of the enjoyment of being in a Sacred Circle is the chance for people to share together in fellowship. Circles with a small group of people can be more fun than a mentor situation because there is a chance to meet and interact with other people.

The meeting should be informative enough to allow people to expand their knowledge and skills on the topic or the event. Within the time allotted for the meeting, the students should be encouraged to learn something, explore something, develop a skill, or learn to improve on an existing skill.

The meeting should also be challenging. By exploring or expanding on new topics, participants should be asked to challenge their current views and ways of thinking and doing things. Only by tackling challenging questions and skills will they expand and grow. When we are challenged to do something just slightly beyond our current level of ability and we have the confidence to feel that we can overcome that challenge, then we learn through that challenge. This means that facilitators must be able to assess the skill level of their participants and be prepared to help out different levels of ability. They must find ways to challenge these different levels but also offer the encouragement and help necessary to learn to overcome the challenges given. When these criteria are met, a participant will feel engaged in the challenge and will enjoy taking on and overcoming that challenge.

The end product of these challenges and of the Circle as a whole is that it will enrich the members. The participant who takes an active role in the meeting will grow as an individual but the group itself will also grow together. Strong bonds that are possible when a group shares similar ideals will be developed and renewed through each meeting. Furthermore, when a group of participants grows together, the facilitator is also enriched. Sometimes the greatest learning takes place in the facilitator herself.

Another aspect of enrichment happens when something is carried out of the class and into everyday life. A good meeting will help the student learn or do something that can be used in the daily activities beyond the Circle. In that way, not only are people enriched but their lives and the lives of the people around them are also enriched. Good teaching of important spiritual principles will expand outwards into the many circles of lives in and around the class.

Attributes Of A Good Facilitator

The focus of most Circle meetings is the facilitator, teacher, or person leading the group.

A Good Facilitator
<ul><li>*Passionate about the topic*</li><li>*Competent with the topic*</li><li>*Connected to the participants*</li><li>*Confident and comfortable*</li></ul>

Leading a Sacred Circle is ultimately dependent upon the facilitator's relationship to her subject, her participants, and herself. A good facilitator should have a passionate love for her goals which comes through in her meetings because she enjoys sharing her knowledge and abilities with others.

She should also be competent in the subject matter or activity. That does not necessarily mean that she needs to be an expert but she should have a good enough grasp on the concepts or principles involved that she can easily relate those things to her participants and be prepared to answer questions about them. Of course, not all facilitators know the answers to all things about any subject and saying "I don't know" is a perfectly acceptable answer to a question–especially if it is followed by the phrase "but I'll find out for you." However, if you find you do not know the answer to the majority of questions being asked then it may be time to review your subject matter further.

Facilitators should also have a strong relationship with their participants. Facilitators work best when they are truly interested in the progress and the contributions of the members of the Circle. Facilitators should be better listeners than talkers and learning the Sacred Listening skills presented in this book can help them develop that skill. Leading Circles is not all that different from counseling except that facilitators have a specific path of learning and experience they want people to follow. Good facilitators are supportive of the developmental process of their members. They actually believe that people can achieve success even when someone does not believe it. Most importantly, their style of support is laced with a light-hearted humor that says they enjoy sharing and relating to their participants.

Good facilitators also have a positive relationship with themselves. They know they may not be total experts or that they have their own faults but they are confident in what they are doing. That confidence comes through experience and through positive feedback from students and formal or informal evaluations. Most of all, excellent facilitators strive to be authentic: they are true to themselves and their students;

they thrive on their own good qualities but are honest about their shortcomings; they are honest to themselves and to others about who they are; and they are generally positive, upbeat, and friendly in and out of the meeting.

Formal Evaluation Questions - *The Environment*

- *Was the space adequate?*
- *Were the furnishings adequate?*
- *Were there any unnecessary distractions?*
- *Was the space clean and comfortable?*
- *Formal Evaluation Questions*

Formal Evaluation Questions - The Meeting

- *Did you enjoy the meeting?*
- *Did you learn something interesting and worthwhile?*
- *Did it meet your expectations?*
- *Did you find the activities too difficult? Too easy?*
- *Did the meeting leave you feeling enriched and excited about what you learned?*
- *What worked well?*
- *What could be improved?*

Formal Evaluation Questions - *The Facilitator*

- *Was the facilitator competent in teaching and running the meeting?*
- *Did the facilitator explain things well?*
- *Did the facilitator relate well to the participants?*
- *Was the facilitator supportive of the participants?*

- *Did the facilitator have a positive attitude throughout the meeting?*
- *Was the facilitator helpful?*
- *What did the facilitator do well?*
- *What could the facilitator have done better?*

Exercise

Solo Exercise

Solo Exercise no. 1 - The Formal Evaluation

1. Draw up a written evaluation form that would be appropriate for your Circle.

2. Be sure to include questions about:

    1. the environment

    2. the meeting

    3. the facilitator

Partner Exercise

Partner Exercise no. 1 - Using the Evaluation

1. Have a practice meeting as was done in the previous chapter.

2. Have the participants practice using the formal evaluation.

3. Discuss the results in with support and compassion.

Chapter Four: Maintenance

Introduction

Care For The Caregiver

U p until now, this book has focused on how a Lay Minister can care for others. Seeing to the needs of others can be a rewarding and fulfilling activity but it can also be exhausting–especially if the caregiver forgets to take care of herself. Caregivers know how important it is to see to the needs of others but often forget to see to their own needs. In this section, we will look at some of the reasons for that and what symptoms can result from the neglect of the self. Finally, we will look at a great way for Lay Ministers to renew themselves through the practice of a spiritual retreat.

Challenges to Caregivers

- *Burnout*
- *Losing hope*
- *Helping too much*
- *Emotional involvement*
- *Isolation*
- *Undefined boundaries*

* _Not taking breaks_

The greatest challenge to caregivers of any religious tradition is burnout. Burnout occurs when someone becomes both exhausted and disillusioned with their work. If burnout is not recognized and treated, it can cause the person to become very negative toward their work and toward life in general and may even lead to personal health problems. Many fine healers have given up their practice due to burnout. Symptoms include a feeling of total exhaustion; irritability with self and others; being highly critical or impatient with others; experiencing frustration, sleeplessness, or depression; becoming withdrawn; not wanting to continue to work, or a loss of a spiritual connection, especially related to the work. The solution to burnout is to seek a balance with yourself between rest, fun, and spiritual work. That balance must be sought at all levels: physical, mental, and emotional, as well as spiritually.

Symptoms of Burnout

* _Exhaustion_
* _Irritability_
* _Becoming highly critical_
* _Becoming withdrawn or ill_

Seeking balance physically should include working to remain physically healthy and fit. Some sort of exercise routine should be included in the life of anyone who wants to stay fit–especially as the years take their natural toll on health. A very minimum effort is to try and do twenty minutes of exercise at least three times a week.

It is also important to take breaks. These include short breaks during long sessions or after short sessions but should also include longer breaks like vacations or spiritual retreats. Time should be set aside for resting and playing as well. A full night of sleep is important to health and balance. The minimum that is usually recommended is 7-8 hours. Along with rest, play too is often neglected but it is important to remember that having fun is not only enjoyable, it is also necessary to maintain balance and health. One needs to eat healthy foods as often as possible without overindulging or skipping meals. All of these are things I am sure that you have heard before.

Most people are familiar with the basics of physical health; the problem is getting people to find the motivation to do them. That motivation can be to avoid burnout. One thing that some people may not be as aware of is that physical balance also requires setting physical boundaries. We will discuss how to do that later in this section.

Physical Balance
• *Keep fit*   • *Take breaks*   • *Rest well*   • *Play*   • *Eat well*

Staying mentally balanced requires that you keep learning about what you do, about your spiritual practice, and about anything that you love. If you think you have learned all that you can about being a good caregiver then you have not learned enough. There will always be more to learn and experience. Be willing to learn about new techniques and practices and be willing to try them out. Be willing to challenge yourself to try new things or to try something different. Take on a more challenging situation even if you think you are not ready quite yet. Try taking your skills to a local hospital or prison. Try anything that might get you out of a rut.

One common problem with being a caregiver is that you give so much of yourself to others that you begin to feel guilty if you do anything for yourself. This can be a dangerous and unhealthy attitude. Just like the people you help deserve to be happy, so do you. Caregivers often help people find joy in their lives but are not willing to do the same for themselves. They may think that taking time to be good to themselves is selfish but being good to yourself and being selfish is not the same thing. You are only being selfish when you do something for yourself that may cause harm or neglect to others. Eating an entire meal by yourself when others around you are hungry is being selfish. Treating yourself to a nice dinner out once in a while is not being selfish. Be good to yourself so that you may be good to others.

Sometimes it also helps to remember why you wanted to help others in the first place. If you can recall the joy and excitement you feel or may have felt when you helped another person improve his life then you may be able to carry that feeling through the more difficult times. Burnout can happen when reality does not meet the expectations of a dream. The hope is that you will always do a great job of being a lay minister, that what you do will enrich the lives of all those you work with, and that everyone will appreciate your wisdom and skill. The reality is that you will make mistakes, not all people can be helped, and not everyone appreciates you and what you do. If the disappointments and frustrations begin to outweigh the rewards, then you may begin to experience burnout. Compliments and positive comments energize you while difficulties deplete you. If you can take time to really appreciate the good moments and learn to accept your failures and shortcomings, you may be able to keep a positive attitude in your work.

Mental Balance
<ul><li>*Learn*</li><li>*Challenge yourself*</li><li>*Avoid guilt*</li><li>*Maintain a positive attitude*</li></ul>

One of the best ways to stay balanced emotionally is to love and be loved. You can do this through a committed relationship of some kind but you can also do it by maintaining contact with those friends and family that care for you and support you. If none of these options are available to you then you will begin to feel isolated. People sometimes become workaholics to avoid the loss of love or other difficulties in life. They attempt to become so involved with their work that they forget about other troubles but the solution rarely works. Either complete exhaustion will occur or the person will still be forced to deal with the difficult situations. There are many ways to seek out friends and lovers. There are affinity groups, spiritual groups, internet groups, and so on. Make the investment in time to meet others. Be genuinely supportive and caring about the people you meet so that they will want to do the same for you. If you find that you are having a hard time making and keeping relationships it may be time to make some adjustments to your personality.

Another important way to seek emotional balance is to find a support person or group for yourself. Just as Seekers need someone to talk to about their frustrations and challenges, caregivers need to do the same. A mentor or a teacher may be someone who can fill that role or you can seek out a group of people who do similar work. There are several organizations that support ministers, counselors, caregivers, and spiritual directors. Some of them are organized around one particular religion but some are not. If you cannot find a suitable group you can always start one of your own. The internet makes it easier for people to connect and form groups though face-to-face discussions are always the best. Only when people are together can they directly share, care, and support each other rather than through just words typed on a keyboard. Besides, hugging a person is always more rewarding than hugging your computer.

Emotional Balance

- *Love*
- *Be loved*
- *Seek support for yourself*

Most people know about the importance of maintaining physical, mental, and emotional balance even if they may not always engage in practices that maintain that balance but fewer seem to know about the importance of maintaining spiritual balance. A deep spiritual practice is more than just something fun and interesting to do. Maintaining spiritual balance is as important as maintaining the balance of any other part of the self; it is part of the balance of the whole self.

When people become busy, often the first thing that gets neglected in their lives is their spiritual practice. I believe that a good spiritual practice, more than anything else, is the one thing that will energize you and help see you through the challenging times. Try to maintain your spiritual practice as you continue your work as a caregiver and if that practice begins to feel as if it is becoming stale then take some time to challenge your practice. Learn about the practices of other traditions and religions or deepen your understanding of your own practice. Try altering your practice somewhat or try another spiritual exercise. You could take a class or go to a different worship experience–anything that will refresh and renew your own practice.

Spiritual Balance

- *Maintain a spiritual practice*
- *Renew your spirituality*
- *Return to nature*

Common Challenges

There are many things that can lead to burnout and disillusionment but in this section, we will discuss a few additional challenges that caregivers often face with some suggestions for finding solutions to each. Those difficulties which are met most often in caring for others include: losing hope, helping too much, getting emotionally involved with Seekers, becoming isolated, not creating boundaries, and not taking breaks. All caregivers experience each of these to some degree and are not necessarily problems unless the ability to care for others or the health and well being of the caregiver becomes diminished.

Losing Hope

Sometimes the task of helping people becomes too daunting and it seems as if all that you are doing is for naught. It is at this point that you may begin to lose hope and give up. This is where clearly defined goals and outcomes for your Seeker are important. Try not to create unrealistic goals for yourself or the people you are helping. Define a larger goal but also create very small and accessible goals that help the Seeker move toward the larger goal. Define success not by the larger goal but by the attainment of much smaller and easier goals. Be realistic and honest with both yourself and with the Seeker. You should also keep in mind that some failure is inevitable.

There are some people who simply cannot or will not be helped. Some maintain their life challenges because they are a defense against truth and a harsh reality. They may call out for help and then may do everything in their power to prevent anyone from actually helping. If you have done the best you can do, then learn to be happy with that and learn to let go. If you have not done the best you can do, then use the experience to learn how to do better next time. It is possible that you are incapable of helping where someone else may be able to do so. You will have strengths and weaknesses as all people do. Learn the ways in which you can be helpful and be able to refer people to others when you cannot help.

Helping Too Much

It would seem to be a strange irony but it is possible for a helper to help too much. You must remember that you are only one person and you only have so much energy to give to others before that energy runs out. You will need to decide how many people you can help at one time and over a period of time. You will need to decide how to take time to care for yourself as well. It is possible to help so much that you ignore the parts of your life that actually excite and energize you. You must be able to charge your own batteries before you can have the energy to assist another person.

The way to do these things is to take inventory of your schedule and workload. If you are feeling overloaded you will need to either reduce your number of tasks or lower the difficulty level of those tasks or do a little of both. Another way to help reduce the problem of helping others too much is to make sure that you are helping yourself. Imagine that you were a Spiritual Advisor for yourself. How would you advise yourself to take it easy and enjoy life?

Emotional Involvement

People who care for others naturally have a big heart. It is the reason that many people choose to become caregivers but getting too emotionally involved in a session or in the lives of others can be draining. It will be necessary for you as an Advisor to maintain some distance between yourself and the Seeker even if that person is a close friend or family member. That is why advising for very close people like family members can be very difficult. Keeping some emotional distance from the Seeker is important because it gives you the room to be objective. As emotional as your Seeker may get, you need to remain calm and rational so that you can truly be helpful.

For that same reason, it is also a good idea not to get emotionally involved with the person you are helping. Seekers come to Advisors in moments of great vulnerability. They may be consciously or unconsciously looking for someone to cling onto for support–or more. It can be easy to take advantage of these feelings and develop an intimate relationship but, again, doing so may not be helpful to the Seeker. It is possible to create a relationship that is codependent which means that the Seeker comes to depend on you to help but you become dependent on the Seeker to need your help. In order to feed the ego or the Advisor's need to be needed, a codependent Advisor will only help a Seeker to a certain degree, thus ensuring that the Seeker will continue to need her help. In such a situation, no one is being helped. In order to prevent these problems, you will need to learn to create emotional distance from the Seeker, learn to define clear goals, and limit the amount of time and number of sessions spent with the Seeker.

Isolation

It is possible to become so wrapped up in the process of caring for others that you forget that your own relationships need their own care. Eventually, you are cut off from friends and family and become isolated. You can also become cut off from other relationships. If you cease to do your own personal spiritual practice you become separated from those things that help you feel connected to your source of strength.

Not Defining Boundaries

Caregivers need to set limits and boundaries for themselves and for the sessions they have with Seekers. Boundaries can help reduce or prevent inappropriate or harmful events from happening and make the life of the Advisor much easier. Boundaries need to be determined by the caregiver before starting sessions and should be made clear to the Seeker. The types of things that need to have clear boundaries are the focus and direction of the session, the manner of the interaction between Advisor and Seeker, and the format of the session. The caregiver should determine what things will be considered beyond the boundaries of discussion and help. Every session should have a focus that is clearly defined and stated during the opening session. Things that go beyond that focus should be limited.

The Lay Minister also needs to have a clear idea of how she should interact with the Seeker. During the session, the relationship should be a caring one, but it must also be a professional one as well. There should be no inappropriate touching or flirting even with people that are considered close. All discussions should be kept confidential to the limits of the law and personal ethics. A level of emotional distance should be maintained so that the caregiver can be objective and she should never become personally involved with the problems of the Seeker.

The format of the session should be clearly defined before beginning any advising and the caregiver needs to adhere to the limits set. There should be a clearly defined starting and ending time and place and there needs to be a policy determined on how often, if at all, the caregiver will meet outside of those defined times. The caregiver should strive to start and end on the times assigned and follow closely the format and timetable designed for the session. Flexibility is important but care needs to be taken that any changes in a session serve to help the Seeker and the Advisor in achieving their intended goals.

Not Taking Breaks

One of the fastest ways to bring about burnout is to stop taking breaks. The body and mind need to rest often. Breaks need to happen at both the micro and macro levels. Small breaks can happen during a session or between sessions. They can happen during the week, the month, and the year so that different levels of respite can occur. Any session that is scheduled to last more than an hour should include some type of short break. For a short while, conversations can take on a lighter tone or the Lay Minister and Seeker may agree to get something to eat or drink. No two sessions should be scheduled back to back without a short break in between. Sessions take a great deal of energy and strength. There needs to be some amount of "down" time afterward. You should have time to reflect and take notes if you wish. At least one part of every week should be set aside for doing spiritual work or for doing personal fun and relaxing activities. Try to also schedule at least one day every month as a full day off.

I suggest that all Lay Ministers and caregivers take a spiritual retreat at least once a year. A well planned and enacted spiritual retreat can be one of the most spiritually uplifting and energizing things that you can do for yourself. During a retreat, the focus is purely on doing spiritual work in order to deepen and strengthen your spiritual connection and practice.

Exercises

Solo Exercise

<u>Solo Exercise no. 1 - Prevention</u>

1. Describe in writing how you plan to prevent the following challenges in your work:

   1. a loss of hope

   2. helping too much

   3. emotional over-involvement

   4. isolation

   5. unclear boundaries

   6. overwork

2. Create a plan for avoiding these problems that can be applied to your work.

Partner Exercise

<u>Partner Exercise no. 1 - Prevention Review</u>

1. Describe your prevention plan to your partner.

2. Discuss its strengths and weaknesses.

3. Make any revisions to the plan you feel are helpful.

Retreats

There are many advantages to personal and group spiritual retreats. They offer a chance to get back to nature and to do some physical movement and exercise. They allow you to focus completely on your spirituality in a way that may be more in depth than is possible at other times. A retreat can be challenging but usually offers chances for some serious rest and relaxation.

The Personal Retreat

A personal spiritual retreat can be a very challenging but highly rewarding form of rest and renewal. The main advantage to doing a personal retreat rather than being part of a group retreat is that you have full control over the planning and activities. Of course, that also means that you have to do all the work.

Planning a Personal Retreat

- *Determine the time frame*
- *Determine the location*
- *Define clear goals and activities*
- *Determine a daily schedule*
- *Create a packing list*

The first step in planning a personal retreat is to choose a time and place and to make any reservations necessary. It is possible to do a spiritual retreat but many find that trying to establish an atmosphere of peacefulness and relaxation at home for an extended period of time is not always possible. Most home environments offer too many distractions and temptations that may lead you astray from your schedule and your spiritual goals. Being on a spiritual retreat requires a good deal of personal discipline. You will need to stay focused on your spiritual goals and not be carried away from day-to-day activities. Being at home reminds you of those things and may not allow you to feel as if you have retreated away from the normal mode of living. If you can manage, it is better to plan a retreat that is away from home–preferably in a place that you consider special or sacred.

There are many retreat centers that can offer you a place to take a personal retreat. Some monasteries offer rooms to rent for just such an occasion. Another option is to simply rent a room in a bed and breakfast or motel. Some rooms can be very inexpensive depending on their location and the time of the year. Since you will not be on a sightseeing tour it will not really matter where you are staying. You will need to eliminate all distractions. Any electronic equipment should be stored or covered up and phones should be turned off. A "Do Not Disturb" sign on the door will help eliminate unwanted interruptions. After finding a place to stay that is suitable, you need to determine how long your retreat will last. I suggest at least a minimum of three days but a week is better–especially for an annual retreat. Some people actually take retreats for a month or longer but, for most people, that is impractical.

The next step in planning a personal retreat is to determine your goals. This is actually one of the most important steps needed to make the retreat a real success because your goals will define what things you will do during the retreat and will help to determine how useful the retreat was to you. There are many things that can be accomplished during a spiritual retreat and can include: making a deeper connection with the divine, getting some needed rest, doing spiritual practices, taking a break from life's routine, contemplating about life and spirituality, renewing your connection with your whole self, or learning to appreciate more fully your own life.

Setting your goals will then help you begin to create a schedule for your retreat. The schedule needs to be balanced so that there is time both for spiritual activities and for rest and reflection. The schedule should reflect the rhythms of your own body. If you know you are more active in the morning and get tired in the early afternoon then plan your activities and rest times accordingly. Each time you do a retreat you will learn better how to schedule things for yourself.

When you have completed your schedule for the retreat then make a list of everything you will need. Be sure to include a food list, a list of cooking and eating utensils (if needed), a list of clothing, a list of materials needed for all your activities and a list of safety precautions. A sample packing list is included in the appendix of this book.

The Retreat Schedule

The following is a sample schedule you can use to help you plan your own retreat. It is based on a five day retreat that includes camping. A schedule such as this should be something to help you focus your day on accomplishing your spiritual goals and should never feel like a burden. You can always make a break or change your plans if you are so moved but it helps to have one planned ahead of time. A more detailed explanation of the listed activities follows at the end of this section.

		Weekly Retreat Schedule
Day One	Morning	arrive and set up
	Afternoon	(follow regular afternoon schedule)
	Evening	(follow regular evening schedule)
Day Two		(follow regular daily schedule)
Day Three	Morning	(follow regular morning schedule)
	Afternoon	special trip
	Evening	complete trip and finish evening schedule
Day Four		(follow regular daily schedule)
Day Five	Morning	(follow regular morning schedule)
	Afternoon	break camp and head home

	n	

The main part of the weekly schedule will be filled by following a daily schedule. The exceptions to this are the times when you arrive and set up your retreat area, during the middle of the week, and when you tear down and clean up your area as you head home. The set up should include time for blessing your retreat space and for making sure that all the activities that will be done during the week will be ready. It is best to do all these preparations on the first day so that you are not using retreat time later in the week. Once your retreat begins, you will want every activity to be spiritual and sacred. The break down should include time for thoroughly cleaning the space and for releasing any feelings created in the space.

In the middle of the week you should schedule a break from the daily routine by planning a special trip or afternoon activity. A long walk or even just an unscheduled afternoon can make for a special time. Whatever activity you choose, it should still feel like it has the same sense of sacredness as your other activities.

	Possible Daily Retreat Schedule	
Morning	6:00 am	wake
	6:30 am	stretching
	7:00 am	meditation/prayer
	8:00 am	meal
	9:00 am	morning ritual/ practice
	10:00 am	quiet time
	11:00 am	walking meditation
Afternoo n	12:00 pm	meal

	1:00 pm	rest
	3:00 pm	sacred reading
	4:00 pm	tea ritual/ceremony
	5:00 pm	special activity
Evening	6:00 pm	meal
	7:00 pm	evening ritual/ practice
	8:00 pm	journaling/ quiet time
	9:00 pm	bed

Personal Retreat Activities

Every part of a spiritual retreat should be treated as a sacred activity from the moment you wake to the time you fall asleep. The following is a list of all the activities that can be done during a retreat. Many of these activities require the participant to act mindfully. That is, to be completely absorbed in the activity itself without distraction. Sometimes it can help to actually think about the activity that you are doing. For example, when dressing in the morning, you can stay mindful of the task of dressing by telling yourself things like "I am now putting on my shirt," or "I am now eating my breakfast." As you do these things, concentrate on the sensations being experienced. As you put on your shirt feel the texture of the shirt against your skin, feel the warmth the shirt brings to your body, smell the (hopefully) clean scent of the shirt, and so on.

I am the first to admit that I am not the type to always clean up after myself. At home, I often do not make the bed or always put my clothes away but during a retreat I am much more conscious of cleaning and putting away things in their assigned locations. The whole point of a retreat is to find some calm in the storm of life. There should always be a sense of calmness, serenity, and order during the retreat. Therefore, I like to have everything clean and stored away in a systematic order when I am on retreat.

Retreat Activities

Mindful Waking

Wake on time (preferably without the help of a loud disturbing alarm clock). Clean yourself then dress slowly and mindfully. Clean up the sleeping area and stow all sleeping gear. Remind yourself of the goals you have set for the retreat and for the day. Offer a brief prayer, blessing, or chant for the day.

Morning Stretch

Stretch your body slowly and mindfully using a stretching routine technique such as Yoga, Tai Chi, or Chi Kung. Be sure to stretch all the major muscle groups of your body.

Sitting Meditation/Prayer

Sit quietly and meditate or pray for at least 20 minutes. An hour would be preferable. You may choose to increase the meditation time each day of the retreat. Choose a preferred method of sitting meditation or prayer and follow that method.

Mindful Eating

The meal should be slowly and mindfully prepared. Offer a prayer or blessing for the meal. While eating the meal, do so slowly and mindfully. Enjoy the food and its smells, textures, and sensations. After the meal, clean the dishes in the same manner as the meal was prepared and eaten. Likewise, clean up after the meal slowly and mindfully. Stow away all food, eating utensils, and cooking gear in their defined locations.

Sacred Rituals/Practices

Prepare your sacred space according to your practice and tradition. Do a sacred ritual or spiritual practice in line with the goals of your retreat. (See the appendix for some suggestions.) End your activity and contemplate on it.

Quiet Time

Find a place to sit quietly and do a simple and quiet activity such as: easy reading, taking a nap, easy contemplation or reflection, simple arts or crafts project, or just relaxing.

Walking Meditation

Take a walk slowly and mindfully in nature. Focus on the breath and on sensing the things around you as you walk. This meditation can take other forms such as:

- Circular Walk - walk slowly in a small circle so that you can concentrate fully on the walking meditation rather than on where to go.

- Blessing Walk - walk through a natural area and bless everything you come across such as the trees, flowers, animals, etc.

- Labyrinth Walk - create a labyrinth on the ground or by using trail flags. Walk slowly and mindfully to the center of the labyrinth. Meditate at its center and then walk back out in the same manner.

- Mindful Hike - walk along a path in a quiet and mindful state. Observe your surroundings with all your senses.

Silent Rest

There is nothing tricky to this one. Just rest or sleep but be sure to remain quiet.

Sacred Reading

Before your retreat you should choose several books. They should be works that can lead to contemplation about spirituality (either yours or others). Slowly and carefully read a section of one of the books you have chosen. Stop to contemplate on any interesting and thoughtful passages. Take notes or write comments. You might choose to journal after reading.

Tea Ceremony

Slowly and mindfully prepare a cup of tea and some light foods. Say a blessing or prayer for the food and tea. Very slowly drink the tea. Enjoy its aroma, feel, and taste. When done, clean all cups, plates, and utensils and stow away all food and cooking items.

Special Activity

Choose something that you personally enjoy doing or something that would help you with your spiritual goals that is not included in any of the other activities. Suggestions for special activities include:

- Musical activities such as chanting, singing, or drumming.
- Crafts such as making prayer beads, knitting, crocheting, origami, etc.
- Art projects such as writing, painting, sculpting, etc.
- Quiet games or puzzles.
- Sacred dance

Journaling

Write notes into a personal journal. Consider answering questions such as:

- What are your goals for this retreat?
- Have you met some of those goals today?
- What activities have you done today?
- What did you learn and experience from each?
- What are your hopes for this part of the retreat?
- What are your fears for this part of the retreat?

- What can you do to further your spiritual goals?

- What other thoughts and feelings have you experienced so far?

Mindful Sleep

Clean your area and stow all equipment for the night. Change into sleeping clothes. Do any evening rituals or practices you may have. Meditate for a few moments on how you have or have not met your spiritual goals for the day and for the retreat. Offer a prayer, blessing, or chant for the evening. Go to sleep.

The Group Retreat

Taking a retreat with a group of people rather than by yourself can be a very different yet still rewarding experience. A group retreat can offer several advantages over a personal retreat. For one thing, being with a group can be less lonely than being by yourself for a week. Activities can be shared and, as we will see, some activities are more effective when done with a group. When other people are in a retreat together there is opportunity for mutual support. When you are alone it is easy to become frustrated and quit or to get off track from your goals. A group of people with similar goals can help each other meet those goals and can offer encouragement when the going gets tough. The disadvantages of a group retreat is that the group needs to take more care in following the schedule together leaving less room for spontaneity (unless the group decides together to change the schedule). Having a group of people do anything together requires more planning and coordination than is usually required for a solo endeavor.

It is also usually more difficult for a group of people to take the same amount of time off together. The schedule I will offer here is for a three day retreat since most people are only able to take an extended weekend together.

Weekend Retreat Schedule		
Friday	03:00 PM	people arrive and set up
	05:00 PM	Opening Ritual/Practice
	06:00 PM	Pot Luck Dinner
	08:00 PM	Fire Circle
Saturday	06:00 AM	Wake
	06:30 AM	Morning Movement
	07:00 AM	Morning Ritual/Practice
	08:00 AM	Breakfast
	08:30 AM	Clean Up
	09:00 AM	Group Meditation/Chanting/ Prayer
	09:30 AM	Quiet Time
	10:00 AM	Walking Meditation
	11:00 AM	Spiritual Reading
	12:00 PM	Lunch
	01:00 PM	Free Time
	01:30 PM	Workshop I
	04:00 PM	Tea Ritual
	04:30 PM	Workshop II
	06:00 PM	Dinner
	07:00 PM	Group Discussion
	08:00 PM	Evening Ritual/Practice
	09:00 PM	Fire Circle
Sunday	Morning	(same as Saturday morning)

	12:00 PM	Lunch
	01:00 PM	Small Groups
	03:00 PM	Closing Ritual/Practice
	04:00 PM	Clean Up and Departure

Group Retreat Activities

Many of the activities listed under the personal retreat section above can be done with a group with little or no additional adjustment. These activities include the morning stretches and movement, the different meditations, quiet time, and the walking meditations. Some activities may need some adoption to work with a group and there are some activities that work well only with a group.

Group Ritual/Practice

The group performs a ritual, ceremony, or other practice according to their own tradition. Different rituals done throughout the weekend may have different purposes. The Opening Ceremony is done on the first evening. In addition to the group's regular routine, additional activities can include:

- A statement of the spiritual goals for the retreat.
- A blessing, prayer and/or purification of the retreat space, the retreat itself, and the participants.
- A dedication by the participants to commit to the goals of the retreat and to help others do the same.
- Consideration of questions for contemplation such as:
  1   What are your hopes for this retreat?
  1   What are your fears about this retreat?
  1   What expectations do you bring?
  1   What personal goals do you hope to accomplish?

- The Morning Ceremony is done early in the morning and can include activities such as:

  A review of goals and commitments of the retreat.

  A reminder of the vow taken to follow the goals.

  A blessing for the day's events and for the participants.

  A chance to ask for strength and spiritual guidance.

  A commitment to a time of silence from the Morning Ceremony through lunch. A vow of silence taken by a group can be a powerful retreat experience in that it requires people to communicate without words and maintain a sense of quiet peacefulness throughout the remainder of the morning events.

- The Evening Ceremony can include the following activities:

  1   Sharing by the participants about what was learned and experienced throughout the day.

  1   A chance to offer gratitude for the day and for those that helped enact the day's events.

  1   Offering gratitude for spiritual guidance.

- The Closing Ceremony is done as the last ritual of the retreat and can include:

  1   A review of what was learned throughout the retreat.

  1   A sharing of experiences by the participants.

  1   A chance to offer gratitude to all those who helped with the retreat.

  1   A chance to offer gratitude for spiritual guidance.

l   A consideration of questions for final contemplation such as:

    l   How were your hopes and fears realized during the retreat?

    l   What did you learn and experience that you will carry with you after the retreat?

    l   How did the retreat fare against your expectations?

    l   Did you accomplish the goals you set for yourself?

Communal Meals

Meals should be done as a group where everyone shares in the responsibilities including preparation, serving, and clean up. Slowly and mindfully prepare the meal. Offer a prayer or blessing for the meal. If the meal is breakfast or lunch under a vow of silence, then there should be no talking during the meal and all other noises should be limited. The vow of silence should end after lunch has been finished by everyone.

After the meal, the group should share in cleaning up. The first dinner on the first evening of the weekend ritual will be the first time that all the participants will sit down together. After the meal is complete, the group may wish to have a meeting to do the following:

- Welcome participants and an introduction of those who will be leading events and who helped plan the retreat.
- Discuss the purpose of the retreat.
- Go over the schedule of the retreat with a brief introduction to the activities.
- Discuss emergency procedures if a problem arises.
- Have an introduction to the materials to be read for the spiritual reading and discussion activities.

The Fire Circle

If the retreat is done in an outdoor location like a campground and a fire is allowed, build a fire for all to gather around. (Be sure to follow all guidelines and rules for fires according to the owners or caretakers of the location.) If a fire is not possible, then the group should gather together in a circle. Fire Circle activities can include:

- conversation
- sacred dancing
- drumming
- chanting and singing
- story and myth telling

Sacred Reading and Discussion

These can actually be one activity or two. The group spends time together reading the spiritual text or material selected ahead of time by the facilitator. The group can either read the text silently to themselves or it can be done by having participants read aloud parts of the text. The reading can be followed by a group discussion based on questions prepared by the facilitator or the group discussion can happen later in the day giving the participants time to think about the text to themselves for a period of time.

Workshops

Facilitators for workshops are chosen before the retreat. Each facilitator chooses a topic for his or her workshop. These topics are reviewed at the first dinner meeting. Depending on the size of the group, more than one workshop can be offered so that people may have a choice. Be sure to allow time for questions and reflection for each workshop.

Group Tea Ritual

A simple act such as drinking tea together can become a sacred ritual. Here is an example of how that can be done. Participants bow to each other and sit quietly for a moment in a circle. The facilitator passes a bowl of tea bags around the circle and offers a blessing. Each person in the circle in turn takes the bowl and selects a tea bag and then passes the bowl to the next person with the same blessing. The facilitator will fill teacups with warm water and pass them one at a time to the next person in the circle. Each person should offer each teacup with a bow and each should be received with a bow until all persons have a filled teacup. The facilitator will then raise his or her tea bag and the others will follow. The leader will offer a blessing. The participants then infuse their tea to their liking but do not drink. The facilitator holds up her cup of tea and offers a final blessing. All drink the tea together. The facilitator begins passing the small treats around the circle in the same manner as before. When all have finished, leader bows to group and group returns the bow.

Group Discussion/Stories

The group gathers together to discuss the spiritual text or reading offered earlier in the day or the group can discuss issues related to the retreat.

Small Group Breakouts

Similar to the workshops, small group activities can be offered by several facilitators. However, these activities are less formal in structure and will require less planning and preparation. Small group activities can include:

- One-on-one or small group sessions.
- Spiritual Advising.
- Spiritual Direction.
- Small discussions of religious topics usually begun by posing a single question to the participants of the session.

Exercises

Solo Exercises

Solo Exercise no. 1 - Personal Retreat Planning

- Plan a week long personal spiritual retreat for yourself.
    - l create the weekly schedule
    - l create the daily schedule with activities
    - l include a packing list

※

Solo Exercise no. 2 - The Personal Retreat

- Take a week long spiritual retreat based on your plans.
- Take notes throughout the retreat.
- After the retreat, review your notes and assess the retreat.
- Consider ways to improve your plans.

※

Solo Exercise no. 3 - Group Retreat Planning

- Plan a weekend group retreat for you and some partners.
    - l create the weekend schedule
    - l create a daily schedule with activities
    - l include a packing list

Partner Exercises

Partner Exercise no. 1 - Group Retreat Planning Review

- Have a group review your plans for a weekend retreat.

- Make any changes based on their suggestions.
- Revise your plan.

❋

Partner Exercise no. 2 - The Group Retreat

- Take a weekend group spiritual retreat based on your plans.
- Take notes throughout the retreat.
- After the retreat, consult your partners for a review.
- Review your notes, review the comments from your partners, and assess the retreat.
- Consider ways to improve your plans.

Appendices

Appendix 1- Taking Notes

Date:	Identifier:
Define The Problem	
Feelings Related to the Problem	
Relationship to Spiritual Connection	
Actions to Take	

Appendix 2 - A List Of Contacts: Individuals

Service	Name	Address	Phone	Email

Counselors			
Ministers			
Doctors			
Social Workers			
Teachers			
Lawyers			
Other			

Appendix 3 - A List Of Contacts: Organizations

Service	Name	Address	Phone	Email
12 Step Groups				
Support				

Groups				
Hotlines				
Other				

Appendix 4 - A List Of Contacts: Agencies

Service	Name	Address	Phone	Email
Child Care				
Shelters				
Women's Services				
Hospice				
Food Banks				
Meal Services				
Elderly Services				

Addiction Center				
Other				

Appendix 5 - Personal Retreat Packing List

[ ] clothes for five days
    [ ] shoes
    [ ] socks
    [ ] pants and shorts
    [ ] shirts
    [ ] under garments
    [ ] hat
    [ ] sweater or sweatshirt
    [ ] coat
[ ] dirty clothes bag
[ ] sunglasses
    [ ] toiletries
    [ ] bathroom items
    [ ] all medications (enough for six days)
    [ ] sunscreen (preferably all natural)
    [ ] bug repellent (preferably all natural)
    [ ] emergency items
    [ ] cell phone
    [ ] first aid kit
    [ ] ritual items
[ ] trail markers
[ ] journal
[ ] pen
[ ] candles
[ ] matches or lighter
[ ] items for making music, dancing, or singing
    [ ] reading materials
        [ ] sacred reading

[ ] other reading
[ ] information
[ ] maps
[ ] directions to retreat location
[ ] money
[ ] food

day one
[ ] dinner

day two
[ ] breakfast
[ ] lunch
[ ] tea
[ ] dinner

day three
[ ] breakfast
[ ] lunch
[ ] tea
[ ] dinner

day four
[ ] breakfast
[ ] lunch
[ ] tea
[ ] dinner

day five
[ ] breakfast
[ ] lunch
[ ] cooking items
[ ] grill or stove
[ ] cooler
[ ] charcoal

[ ] propane
[ ] dishes and utensils
[ ] cups
[ ] matches
[ ] can opener
[ ] bottle opener
[ ] trash bags
[ ] dish soap
[ ] dish towels
[ ] camping equipment
[ ] tent
[ ] sleeping bags
[ ] air mattress
[ ] blankets
[ ] pillows
[ ] other
[ ] chair
[ ] propane lamp
[ ] towels
[ ] paper and pen
[ ] batteries
[ ] backpack or day pack
[ ] camping knife
[ ] camera

Appendix 6 - Stretching Routine

The following is a simple upper body stretching routine that can also be done as a spiritual meditation. Concentrate on gently stretching and relaxing your muscles while you connect with the space around you.

- **Reach Up**. To begin this basic routine, stand with your feet together (about shoulder width) with your arms at your side. Bring your arms up over your head and reach up while looking up. Feel the stretch in your back and front as well as in your arms and neck. Lift your head so that you feel the stretch along your spine and into your neck.

Pull your arms and feel the stretch throughout them. Spread your fingers and turn your palms up so that you feel the stretch in your hands and fingers.

- **Bend Down**. Bend down slowly until you feel the stretch in your back and legs. Go only as far as you can until you just begin to feel the stretch. If you can, bend all the way down and touch the floor but do not attempt to do so if it is not comfortable. Try to bend as far as you can with your legs straight. Keep your knees straight but do not lock them. If this is difficult for you then bend the knees slightly as you bend down. When you are done return to your standing position.

- **Reach Forward**. Turn your palms outward and bend forward to about a 90-degree angle. Let your head point down. Stretch your back, shoulders, and neck. When you are done let your hands return to your side and return to your standing position.

- **Reach Right**. Bring your left hand up over your head. Bend your body to your right with your left hand pointing to the right over your head and your right hand at your side with fingers pointing down. Feel the stretch in your left side and neck. Return to your standing position.

- **Reach Back**. Bring both hands up above your head. Bend back slightly until you feel a stretch in your stomach and your upper back. Point your fingers to the space behind you and let your head lift up. Do not drop your head back since this is not a good position for your head. Instead, look straight up and feel the stretch in your neck and shoulders. Return to your standing position.

- **Reach Left**. Bring your right hand over your head then bend to the left in the same way that you bent to the right. Return to your standing position.

- **Standing**. Bring your hands together in a prayer position.

Turn slightly to each side. Return to the center then stand comfortably for a few moments.

Appendix 7 – Bibliography

Introduction

1. McBrien, Richard P. Ministry: A Theological, Pastoral Handbook. 1987, Harper and Row.

2. Nouwen, Henri M. Creative Ministry. 1971, Image Books.

Chapter 1

1. Borris-Dunchanstang, Eileen R. Finding Forgiveness: A 7-Step Program for Letting Go of Anger and Bitterness. 2006, McGraw-Hill.

2. Clinebell, Howard. Basic Types of Pastoral Care and Counseling: Resources for the Ministry of Healing and Growth.1984, Abingdon Press.

3. Grof, Stanislav and Christina Grof. Spiritual Emergency: When Personal Transformation Becomes A Crisis. 1989, Jeremy P. Tarcher.

4. Guiley, Rosemary Ellen. Dreamwork for the Soul. 1998, Berkley Books.

5. Hauck, Paul A. Overcoming Worry and Fear. 1975, Westminster John Knox Press.

6. Jones, Carol D. Overcoming Anger: How To Identify It, Stop It, and Live a Healthier Life. 2004, Adams Media Publications.

7. Kornfeld, Margaret. Cultivating Wholeness: A Guide

to Care and Counseling in Faith Communities. 1998, Continuum International Publishing Group.

8. Kennedy, Eugene and Sara C. Charles. On Becoming A Counselor: A Basic Guide for Nonprofessional Counselors and Other Helpers. 2001, Crossroad Publishing

9. Kovach, Kimberly K. Mediation. 2003, West Group.

10. McNish, Jill L. Transforming Shame: A Pastoral Response. 2004, Haworth Press.

11. Moursund, Janet and Maureen C. Kenny. The Process of Counseling and Therapy. 2002, Prentice Hall.

12. Rosen, David. Transforming Depression. 2002, Nicolas-Hays Inc.

13. Savage, John. Listening and Caring Skills: A Guide for Groups and Leaders. 1996, Abingdon Press.

14. Silf, Margaret. Wise Choices: A Spiritual Guide to Making Life's Decisions. 2007, Blue Bridge Books.

15. Sperry, Len. Transforming Self and Community: Revisioning Pastoral Counseling and Spiritual Direction. 2002, The Liturgical Press.

16. Stone, Howard W., ed. Strategies for Brief Pastoral Counseling. 2001, Fortress Press.

Chapter 2

1. Anderson, Keith R., and Randy D. Deese. Spiritual Mentoring: A Guide For Seeking and Giving Direction. 1999, InterVarsity Press.

2. Addison, Howard A. Show Me Your Way: The

Complete Guide to Exploring Interfaith Spiritual Direction. 2000 Skylight Paths Publishing.

3. Barry, William and William J. Connolly. The Practice of Spiritual Direction. Harper San Francisco.

4. Farrington, Debra K. Living Faith Day By Day. 2000, Berkley Publishing Group.

5. Fontana, David. The Secret Language of Symbols. 2003, Chronicle Books.

6. Fowler, James W. Stages of Faith: the Psychology of Human Development and the Quest for Meaning. 1981, Harper and Row.

7. Goleman, Daniel. Emotional Intelligence: Why It Can Matter More Than IQ. 2005, Bantam Books.

8. Harrow, Judy. Spiritual Mentoring: A Pagan Guide. 2002, ECW Press.

9. Helminiak, Daniel. Spiritual Development: An Interdisciplinary Study. 1987, Loyola University Press.

10. Kegan, Robert. The Evolving Self: Problem and Process in Human Development. 1982, Harvard University Press.

11. Lebacqz, Karen and Joseph Driskill. Ethics and Spiritual Care: A Guide for Pastors, Chaplains, and Spiritual Directors. 2000, Abingdon Press.

12. Peters, Maggie. Dreamwork: Using Your Dreams as a Way to Self-Discovery and Personal Development. 2001, Gaia Books.

13. Rogers, Carl R. On Becoming A Person. 1961, Houghton-Mifflin.

14. Selby, John and Zachary Selig. Kundalini

Awakening: A Gentle Guide to Chakra Activation and Spiritual Growth. 1992, Bantam Books.

15.   Underhill, Evelyn. Mysticism: The Nature and Development of Spiritual Consciousness. 1993, Oneworld Publications.

16.   Walsh, Roger. Essential Spirituality: Seven Central Practices to Awaken Heart and Mind.

17.   Wilbur, Ken. Integral Spirituality. 2006 Integral Books.

Chapter 3

1. Brookfield, Stephen D., and Stephen Preskill. Discussion as a Way of Teaching. 1999, John Wiley and Sons.

2. Brooks-Harris, Jeff E. and Susan R. Stock-Ward. Workshops: Designing and Facilitating Experiential Learning. 1999, Sage Publications.

3. Draves, William A. How To Teach Adults. 1984, Learning Resources Network.

4. Turner, Nathan W. Leading Small Groups. 1996, Judson Press.

5. Vella, Jane. Learning To Listen, Learning To Teach. 2002, Jossey Bass.

Chapter 4

1. Cooper, David A. Silence, Simplicity and Solitude: A Complete Guide to Spiritual Retreat. 1999, Skylight Paths Publishing.

2. Faulkner, Brooks R. Burnout In Ministry. 1981,

Broadman Press.

About The Author

Kenneth P. Langer

Rev. Dr. Kenneth P. Langer is an ordained Universalist minister and a former college professor with graduate degrees in both music and theology. He is a published writer, composer, and poet and is the author of several works of fiction as well as books on spiritual living. He also enjoys playing and designing games.

Learn more by visiting his website: http://kennethplanger.com

Other Books

Non-Fiction

- Spirituality
  - A Different Calling: A Manual for Lay Ministers and Other Non-Professional Facilitators of Any Spiritual Tradition
  - Many Leaves, One Tree: A Collection of Aphorisms Inspired by the Tao Te Ching
  - The Purpose Derived Life: What In The Universe Am I Here For?
  - Three Guidelines for Ethical Living
  - Playing Cards and the Game of Living Well
  - The Emergence of God: The Intersection of Science, Nature, and Spirituality
  - The Langer Deck
  - Emergent Spirituality: Principles and Practices at the Intersection of Science, Nature, and Spirituality
  - Open Hearts and Open Doors: Radical Hospitality in the Church
  - Let Us Wander: A Ministry of Music and Arts
- Games
  - 52 New Card Games (For Those Old Cards)
  - 36 New Dice Games
  - 40 Games for Forty Dice
  - Castle Imbroglio: An Escape Adventure Book
- Music
  - A Guide to the Art of Musical Performance

- A Theory for All Music
  - Book 1: Fundamentals
  - Book 2: Chords and Part-Writing
  - Book 3: The Tools of Analysis
  - Book 4: Parametric Analysis
- Rounds and Canons for Peace and Justice
- Music for Unitarian-Universalist Choirs
- Songs of Worship
- 50 Songs for Meditation

Fiction

- Science Fiction
  - The Milleran Cluster Series
    - Of Eternal Light
    - The Forever Horizon
    - The Suicide Fire
    - The Song of the Mother
    - The Journey of Awri
- Theater
  - Four Comedies
  - 10 x 10: Ten Ten-Minute Plays Book 1
  - 10 x 10: Ten Ten-Minute Plays Book 2
  - 10 x 10: Ten Ten-Minute Plays Book 3
  - 10 x 10:Ten Ten-Minute Plays Book 4
  - Ageless Wisdom: Multigenerational Plays for Worship
- Poetry
  - Looking At The World: A Collection of Poetry

  - Prayers

Final Note

Thank you for reading this book!

If you enjoyed reading it please let me know
and please consider writing a positive online review.

Ken Langer

Contact Information
personal website: http://kennethplanger.com
book site: http://brassbellbooks.com

www.ingramcontent.com/pod-product-compliance
Lightning Source LLC
LaVergne TN
LVHW011325080426
835513LV00006B/204